Talk about *refreshing*

DRINK
Coca-Cola

Coca-Cola

THE COOKBOOK

THE COOKBOOK

An Hachette UK Company

www.hachette.co.uk

First published in Great Britain in 2013 by Hamlyn,

a division of Octopus Publishing Group Ltd

Endeavour House, 189 Shaftesbury Avenue,

London WC2H 8JY

www.octopusbooks.co.uk

www.octopusbooksusa.com

Distributed in the USA by Hachette Book Group USA,

237 Park Avenue, New York, NY 10017, USA

Distributed in Canada by Canadian Manda Group,

165 Dufferin Street, Toronto, Ontario, Canada M6K 3H6

ISBN 978-0-600-62350-2

Printed and bound in China

10 9 8 7 6 5 4 3 2

Note Guideline Daily Amounts, or GDAs, are a guide to how
many calories and nutrients people can consume each day for a
healthy, balanced diet. Please note that an individual's nutritional
requirements can vary with gender, weight, activity levels, and
age, meaning some people may need to eat more and others less.

CONTENTS

things go better with Coke

TRADE-MARK ®

Coca-Cola

THE STORY

A refreshing creation

Above: Dr. John S. Pemberton, inventor of Coca-Cola.

In Atlanta, Georgia, in 1886 Dr. John Stith Pemberton, pharmacist and inventor of medicines and beverages, made a fragrant, caramel-colored syrup in a brass pot kettle in his backyard. He experimented with different ingredients and, by May of that year, had perfected his creation. He took a pitcher of it to Jacobs' Pharmacy, which was situated just a few doors away, where it was combined in a glass with carbonated water and ice and placed on sale at the soda fountain for 5 cents per glass.

Above: An early photograph shows three women at a soda fountain in New Orleans, Louisiana, in 1887.

Soda fountains offered respectable alternatives to bars as meeting places and sold a variety of food and cold nonalcoholic drinks, such as root beer and beverages flavored with fruit or made with ice cream, and now, in 1886, Atlanta's largest soda fountain also served Coca-Cola.

The now famous name Coca-Cola was one that Dr. Pemberton's partner and bookkeeper, Frank M. Robinson, suggested, saying that "the two Cs would look well in advertising." He is also credited with writing the famous script logo that is still in use today, largely unchanged, for which he adapted the elaborate Spencerian script style that was in common use at the time.

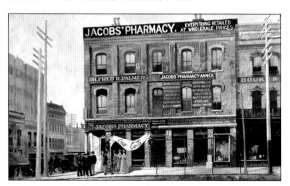

Above: Jacobs' Pharmacy, in Atlanta, Georgia, was the earliest establishment to sell Coca-Cola.

Delicious!
Refreshing!
Exhilarating!
Invigorating!

An oilcloth sign—the first advertising banner for Coca-Cola—was soon attached to the outside of Jacobs' Pharmacy, telling people to "Drink Coca-Cola," and soon the first newspaper advertisement appeared in the the *Atlanta Journal*, declaring: "Coca-Cola. Delicious! Refreshing! Exhilarating! Invigorating!".

By the end of that year, Dr. Pemberton had sold 25 gallons (95 liters) of syrup at a dollar a gallon and an average of nine glasses of Coca-Cola per day were sold. During the first year of sales, Dr. Pemberton spent twice as much money advertising and promoting his product than he earned from it.

In 1887, Dr. John Pemberton registered his "Coca-Cola Syrup and Extract" label as a copyright with the U.S. Patent Office and, in that same year, the first coupons offering people a free glass of Coca-Cola were issued as a marketing device.

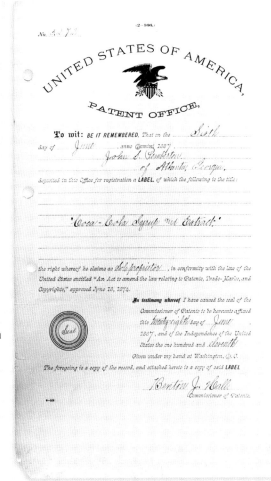

Above: The patent document given to sole proprietor Dr. John Pemberton on registration of his "Coca-Cola Syrup and Extract" label as a copyright with the U.S. Patent Office in 1887.

Asa Candler

Because of failing health, Dr. Pemberton gradually sold parts of his business to various partners and, just before he died in 1888, sold his remaining interest in Coca-Cola to Asa Griggs Candler. Like Pemberton, Candler was a pharmacist. He was also a man with excellent business acumen, achieving sole ownership of Coca-Cola at a cost of $2,300 in 1891.

Above: The Coca-Cola Company founder, Asa Candler.

With all new products, the challenge is getting people to try them. Determined to promote the drink and expand on Dr. Pemberton's marketing, Asa Candler offered a free sample of Coca-Cola. He sent letters and coupons inviting people to soda fountains to try a complimentary glass of Coca-Cola, and it worked wonderfully: Between 1894 and 1913, a staggering number—more than 8.5 million of these coupons—were redeemed.

Spreading the word

Alongside coupons, a vast array of items promoting Coca-Cola began to appear in the 1890s. These included calendars, clocks, trays, porcelain urns for dispensing the syrup, scales, postcards, playing cards, and paper fans. People saw the name everywhere and, by 1892, sales of Coca-Cola syrup were up nearly tenfold.

Asa Candler, together with his brother John S. Candler, Pemberton's former partner Frank Robinson, and two others, formed a Georgia corporation called The Coca-Cola Company in 1892, and the trademark "Coca-Cola" was registered with the United States Patents Office in January 1893.

Above: One of the popular sampling coupons from the 1890s.

By 1895, there were syrup-manufacturing plants in Chicago, Dallas, and Los Angeles and Candler was able to say in his annual report that "Coca-Cola is now drunk in every state and territory in the United States."

The first building—three stories high—erected exclusively as Coca-Cola's headquarters and used for syrup production and to house the management of business, went up in 1898. Candler declared it to be "sufficient for all our needs for all time to come", but, in fact, the flourishing company quickly outgrew it and the Company was to move to new headquarters no fewer than five times in the following 12 years.

Bottling begins

Mississippi businessman Joseph A. Biedenharn, who had been selling Coca-Cola at his soda fountain since 1890, was the first to put it into bottles in 1894. He installed bottling equipment at the back of his store and began delivering cases of bottled Coca-Cola to remote farms and lumber camps along the Mississippi River. He sent 12 of the bottles to Candler, who was, however, reluctant to embrace the idea of Coca-Cola bottles, having built an enormously successful business based on selling the syrup at soda fountains.

Above: Employees pose for a photograph outside The Coca-Cola Company's Atlanta headquarters in 1898.

In 1899, two lawyers from Chattanooga, Tennessee—Benjamin F. Thomas and Joseph B. Whitehead—secured from Asa Candler the rights to bottle and sell Coca-Cola nearly everywhere in the United States for the sum of only one dollar. The first bottling plant opened in Chattanooga later that year. Asa Candler, however, wisely retained the sole rights to the production of Coca-Cola syrup.

A new century

In 1900, music hall actress Hilda Clark became the first celebrity to be used in Coca-Cola advertising, appearing on posters, trays, and even bookmarks. In the same year, Benjamin Thomas and Joseph Whitehead, now joined in business by fellow Chattanooga businessman John T. Lupton, opened a second bottling plant in Atlanta.

Around the same time, they realized they needed more capital to take the bottling operation across the United States. Their solution was to partner with local entrepreneurs to establish Coca-Cola bottling operations. As a testament to the resounding success of portable Coca-Cola, between 1899 and 1909, 379 bottling plants opened. Success brought with it imitators, however, who were eager to emulate the achievements of Coca-Cola and some early advertisements warned customers to "Accept no substitutes."

In 1903, The Coca-Cola Company bought its first motorized vehicle to make deliveries and advertise its product and, in 1911, the advertising budget was more than one million dollars. The company came up with more ways to promote the increasingly popular beverage and, by 1913, Coca-Cola was distributed by 2,300 wholesalers to more than 415,000 retailers. The number of bottling plants grew to more than 1,000, the majority locally owned and operated.

*"**Enjoy a Glass of Liquid Laughter**"*
1911 ADVERTISING SLOGAN

Above: Coca-Cola's history of using celebrities in advertising began with singer Hilda Clark, seen here in a poster from 1903.

Asa Candler bows out

In 1916, Asa Candler retired from The Coca-Cola Company and successfully ran for mayor of Atlanta. In 1919, he sold the company for 25 million dollars—not a bad return on the original $2,300 he had invested in it.

THE SECRET FORMULA

The fabled secret formula for Coca-Cola is one of the most closely guarded trade secrets in history. It all began with Dr. John Pemberton, who went to great lengths to keep what it takes to make Coke a mystery, sharing the recipe with only a small group of people and never writing it down.

When he became sole proprietor of Coca-Cola, Asa Candler went even farther to protect the secrecy of the formula. He scratched off the labels on containers of the various ingredients that went into it and, instead, identified them only by numbers.

In 1898, the company moved to new headquarters on Edgewood Drive in Atlanta, where the secret formula was made in a triangle-shaped room secured by a combination lock on the door. In the early 1900s, Asa Candler taught his son, Charles Howard, to make the secret formula, but it was still never committed to paper.

In 1919, Ernest Woodruff, leading a group of investors buying The Coca-Cola Company from Asa Candler and his family, needed collateral for a loan to finance the purchase of the company. He asked Charles Howard Candler to write down the formula for the first time, to serve as that collateral. This record was placed in a vault in the Guaranty Bank in New York.

In 1925, the loan was repaid and Robert Woodruff, who was by this time president of the company (see pages 14–15 for more about Robert Woodruff), traveled to New York in person to reclaim the secret formula. He placed it in a vault in the Trust Company Bank in Atlanta, where it was to remain for 86 years.

On December 8, 2011, the envelope containing the formula was moved to a giant purpose-built vault at the World of Coca-Cola in Atlanta.

The Woodruff years

In 1919 The Coca-Cola Company was bought by a group of investors headed by Ernest Woodruff and W. C. Bradley. The business was reincorporated and 500,000 shares were sold for $40 a share. Four years later, Ernest's son, 33-year-old Robert W. Woodruff, an experienced businessman who had worked his way up to the position of vice president of the White Motor Company, was elected president of Coca-Cola. This was the beginning of what were to be more than 60 years of leadership by Robert Woodruff, who was president from 1923–1939 and served as chairman of the board from 1939–1942 and 1952–1954. As a man who saw opportunities for expansion everywhere, he probably has had more influence on the company than anyone else.

Above: The Coca-Cola Company president, Robert W. Woodruff.

Taking Coca-Cola home

Under Woodruff's leadership the business reached new heights of success. One of his key concepts was the idea that *Coca-Cola should always be within an arm's reach of desire*. Recognizing the huge potential of bottled Coca-Cola, Woodruff targeted advertising and marketing at encouraging people to enjoy Coca-Cola at home. The company introduced what was then a revolutionary six-bottle carton in 1923, so it was easier for people to carry Coke home with them. This was such an innovation that the company patented it the following year.

By the end of 1928, sales of bottled Coca-Cola exceeded soda fountain sales for the first time. In the early 1930s, teams of women were employed to go door to door in major cities, telling people about the convenient carry-home cartons and offering to install free wall-mounted bottle openers in their kitchens as a handy way to open their Coke bottles.

Above: A sign advertising the handy six-bottle carton introduced in 1923.

You can trust its quality

One of Woodruff's important goals was to make sure that Coke was seen as something to rely on and have confidence in, guaranteeing that customers, wherever they were, got a consistent drink and service every time. Coca-Cola sent out trained technical teams to visit soda fountains around the country, cleaning and repairing equipment and giving soda fountain operators tips on how to mix and serve the perfect glass of Coca-Cola.

And, as another way of spreading the message, these teams were also equipped with supplies of posters and other advertising material, backed up by the slogan "You Can Trust Its Quality," which they gave to soda fountain operators to display.

Working with bottlers, the company established quality standards for the bottling business, too. By 1941, traveling laboratories were set up to go around the United States to make sure that quality standards were maintained at bottling plants.

In 1950, Coca-Cola became the first commercial product to appear on the front cover of *Time* magazine. The magazine had wanted to show a photograph of Robert Woodruff, in recognition of his achievements in driving the company forward; however, he declined, saying that the product was the most important aspect of The Coca-Cola Company.

"Around the corner from everywhere"

1927 ADVERTISING SLOGAN

Above: Published in the *Saturday Evening Post* in 1930, this ad shows a young couple in a pushcart being served glasses of Coca-Cola by a soda jerk against the backdrop of the Atlantic City Boardwalk.

Going global

The spread of Coca-Cola around the world began when Asa Candler's son, Charles Howard Candler, took a gallon (3.8 liters) of syrup with him on a trip to Europe in 1900 and the owner of a London soda fountain placed a modest order for 5 gallons (19 liters). Also in 1900, Coca-Cola was sold in Cuba and Puerto Rico. In 1906, bottling began in Canada, Cuba, and Panama—the first three countries outside the United States to bottle Coke—and, in 1919, the first European bottling plants opened in France. It was under the leadership of Robert W. Woodruff, however, that Coca-Cola really began to spread around the globe.

Above: This 1949 Australian advertisement reflects the global spread of Coca-Cola.

The export bottle

Above: The Foreign Department of Coca-Cola developed a distinctive bottle design for the export market in the late 1920s.

In 1926, the Foreign Department was formed within The Coca-Cola Company to supply syrup to overseas bottlers of the drink. In 1930, the department became a subsidiary of the company, called The Coca-Cola Export Corporation, whose remit was to market the drink outside the United States.

To help promote Coca-Cola in other countries a stylish, special bottle, the Export Bottle, was created. These green bottles, with elegant labels and gold foil wrapped around the top, were designed to resemble Champagne bottles and were shipped around the world.

Countries in which bottling began during the 1920s include Colombia, Belgium, Bermuda, Haiti, Italy, Germany, Holland, Spain, and Mexico. From the mid-1940s to 1960, the number of countries with bottling operations nearly doubled and, by 1957, sales outside the United States accounted for approximately 33 percent of the company's revenue.

INTERNATIONAL MILESTONES

1895   Coca-Cola is sold in every state and territory in the United States

1900   Coca-Cola appears in England, Cuba, and Puerto Rico for the first time

1906   Bottling begins in Canada, Cuba, and Panama

1912   Bottling operations start in the Philippines, the first country in Asia to sell Coca-Cola

1917   Bottling operations start on the island of Guam

1919   The first European bottling plants are opened in Paris and Bordeaux, France

1926   The Coca-Cola Foreign Department is formed

1938   Coca-Cola enters Australia, Austria, Norway, and South Africa

1947   Shanghai is the first city outside the United States to sell more than a million cases of Coke

1948   Coca-Cola is introduced in Egypt

1968   Bottling operations begin in Hungary, the Somali Republic, and Yugoslavia

1972   Bottling begins in Poland

1981   The first bottling plant opens in China. By 2010, there are more than 40

1985   Bottling begins in Russia

1990   Coke is sold in East Germany for the first time since the collapse of the Berlin Wall

2012   The Coca-Cola Company announces it will resume business in Myanmar after a 60-year absence

Above and right: These mid-century magazine ads show how international Coke had become.

New challenges

Alongside everyone else, the company had to deal with the shortfalls that rationing—particularly rationing of sugar—presented, but, despite this, World War II was to bring great opportunities as well as challenges.

In 1941, the United States entered the war and more than one million American troops were mobilized. Although Coca-Cola was by now bottled in 44 countries—on both sides of the conflict—many GIs were stationed in places where it wasn't available. Robert W. Woodruff promised that every man in uniform would get a bottle of Coca-Cola for 5 cents, wherever he was and whatever it would cost the Company—5 cents being the price of a bottle of Coke in the United States at the time.

Spurred on by this, company engineers rose to the occasion. They developed plans for bottling plants that could be shipped to foreign countries and set up as close as possible to combat areas. The first of these was set up in Algeria in 1943 and was followed by 63 others in Europe and the Pacific. The shipping and setting up of these bottling plants was supervised by 148 Coca-Cola employees called technical observers, or TOs. These men had U.S. Army officers' rank, pay, and uniforms—with a patch on them identifying them as Coca-Cola TOs.

Above: Four smiling friends in military uniform sip Coke in this wartime advertisement.

A special request

On June 29, 1943, General Dwight D. Eisenhower's North African headquarters sent an urgent telegram requesting three million bottles of Coke plus materials and equipment to set up bottling plants capable of producing six million bottles of Coca-Cola a month for troops fighting in North Africa. This request came with the proviso that the Coke and equipment should not displace any other military cargo when it was shipped.

Getting Coca-Cola to soldiers fighting in remote areas of the South Pacific was one of the most problematic for the TOs, so they developed a portable dispensing unit, dubbed a "jungle fountain," that could be transported by truck to almost any location and more than 1,000 of these were used during the war.

In all, more than five billion bottles of Coke were consumed by military personnel during World War II. However, the overseas bottling plants, developed to serve American soldiers, had another effect: They also introduced local people to their first taste of Coca-Cola and, when the conflict ended, the bottling plants stayed.

Back home, the company recognized the major role women played in the war—advertising and promotional items depicted patriotic images of women in military uniform and working in factories supplying the war effort.

Right: This 1940s ad announces that 'Coca-Cola delicious and refreshing has arrived in Casablanca!'

Below: Two American soldiers are shown at a portable 'jungle fountain' in the Philippines in this 1945 advertisement.

Coca-Cola

délicieux et rafraîchissant est arrivé à Casablanca !

Le désaltérant de renommée mondiale est maintenant en vente dans toute la ville

Step right up, amigos ... Have a Coke

...Yank friendliness comes back to Leyte

Sports sponsorships

The Coca-Cola Company has a long history of sponsoring major sporting events and organizations, the biggest of which is the Olympic Games.

Sponsoring success

Coca-Cola's involvement with the Olympic Games goes back to 1928, and the company is the longest continuous supporter of the Olympic Games, both Summer and Winter, the Paralympics, and, since 1992, the Olympic Torch Relay. On August 1, 2005, Coca-Cola and the International Olympic Committee announced the renewal of the partnership for 12 years, up to 2020.

Coca-Cola was also a founding partner of the Special Olympics, when Eunice Kennedy Shriver founded the organization in 1968. The Special Olympics provides sports training and athletic competition in a variety of Olympic-type sports for adults and children with intellectual disabilities.

OLYMPIC GAMES HIGHLIGHTS

For the Amsterdam 1928 Olympic Games—the first to have athletics and gymnastics events for women—a ship delivered both the United States Olympic Team and 1,000 cases of Coca-Cola to the Netherlands. The drink

Above: Coca-Cola was one of the three official beverage sponsors at the Los Angeles 1932 Olympics Games, officially known as the "Games of the Xth Olympiad".

was sold at kiosks around the Olympic Stadium, staffed by attendants wearing special coats and caps bearing the Coca-Cola trademark.

For the Helsinki 1952 Olympic Games, which took place before Finland had a Coca-Cola bottler, 30,000 cases of Coke were shipped from Amsterdam aboard a reconditioned World War II landing craft, MS *Marvic*. At the Olympic Winter Games in Oslo that same year, a Norwegian bottler rented a helicopter to advertise Coca-Cola. Most Norwegians had never seen a helicopter and it was later given to the city to use to direct traffic.

For the Tokyo 1964 Olympic Games, Coca-Cola produced a Japanese–English phrasebook that proved so popular with spectators that the company produced a phrasebook for the Mexico City 1968 Olympic Games, the Munich 1972 Olympic Games, and the Olympic Winter Games in Sapporo in 1972 and Nagano in 1998.

For the Montreal 1976 Olympic Games, The Coca-Cola Company bought a horse, named Regardez, and donated it to the Canadian equestrian team, and the company became the first sponsor of the Olympic Museum, which was opened in 1993 in Lausanne, Switzerland.

Above: A Coca-Cola kiosk sells drinks at the Olympic Stadium at the Amsterdam 1928 Olympic Games.

Above: Visitors queuing to visit the Olympic Village at the Mexico City 1968 Olympic Games enjoy some refreshment while they wait.

THE NUMBER 1 OLYMPIC GAMES SPECTATOR SPORT

Dubbed "the number 1 Olympic Games spectator sport," pin trading is a phenomenon that attracts huge amounts of interest at every Olympic Games as countless collectors—known as "pinheads"—get caught up in a frenzy of buying and swapping Olympic Games enameled lapel pins.

The pins depict everything from individual sports and events, committees, and countries to official mascots, corporate sponsors, and countdown days.

The Calgary 1988 Olympic Games saw the first Coca-Cola Official Olympic Games Pin Trading Center, which attracted more than 17,000 visitors each day. At the Albertville, France 1992 Olympic Winter Games, the main trading center was joined by a satellite center and two traveling Coca-Cola "PinMobiles" for more than 350,000 collectors who traded about 1.2 million pins. By the Sydney 2000 Olympic Games, there was so much interest in pin trading that Coca-Cola opened a temporary pin-trading kiosk in Sydney six months before the Olympic Games began. The London 2012 Olympic Games attracted the collectors, both experienced and novice, among spectators and competitors, all eager to acquire some of the 2,012 pins designed specifically for the event. Coca-Cola had two busy trading centers, one in the Olympic Park and the other in Hyde Park in the center of London.

Above: A Coca-Cola pin from the Beijing 2008 Olympic Games. This was the first time that Coca-Cola had a pin-trading centre exclusively for athletes and officials.

Other sporting connections

Alongside the Olympic Games, Coca-Cola has a number of other sports sponsorships, the most well known being FIFA and NASCAR.

FIFA

In 1974, the international soccer/football body FIFA (*Fédération Internationale de Football Association*) and The Coca-Cola Company made history with the first formal agreement between a sports association and a commercial company. Coca-Cola became an official sponsor of the FIFA World Cup™ in 1978, making the company one of FIFA's longest-standing corporate partners. Coca-Cola sponsors all FIFA tournaments, and this sponsorship will extend to 2022.

Leading up to the 2010 FIFA World Cup™ in South Africa, Coca-Cola organized for the second time a global tour of the FIFA World Cup™ Trophy. The tour visited 94 cities in 84 countries, including 50 countries across the African continent. Nearly one million fans had souvenir photos taken with the FIFA World Cup™ Trophy in the largest experiential marketing tour ever undertaken by Coca-Cola. During the tournament itself, every time players celebrated a goal with a dance, Coca-Cola donated $1,500.00 to its "Water for Schools" campaign to provide schools in Africa with access to safe drinking water.

NASCAR

Stock car racing has been dubbed "America's favorite sport". Coca-Cola has been involved with the National Association of Stock Car Auto Racing (NASCAR) for over 50 years, and has been the Official Soft Drink partner of NASCAR since 1998. Well known to every NASCAR fan is the Coca-Cola Racing Family—a group of top drivers that has included past champions Dale Earnhardt, Sr. Bill Elliot, Dale Jarrett, Bobby Labonte, Kurt Busch, and Tony Stewart. The company also sponsors the Coca-Cola 600—an annual 600-mile (965-kilometer) race held in Concord, North Carolina, which has been a key event on the stock car racing calendar since 1960.

Above: Tony Stewart, a member of the Coca-Cola Racing Family, celebrates another victory at Homestead-Miami Speedway in 2011.

Above: *At the Circus* (1939)　Above: *It's a Wonderful Life* (1946)　Above: *Lolita* (1962)

The Reel Thing

At The Circus (1939), *It's a Wonderful Life* (1946), *Lolita* (1962), *The Way We Were* (1973), *9 to 5* (1980), *Strictly Ballroom* (1992), *Independence Day* (1996), *You've Got Mail* (1998), *Million Dollar Baby* (2004), *Casino Royale* (2006), and *The Help* (2011)—what these famous movies have in common is that they all feature Coke in one way or another.

Star of the screen

The iconic Coca-Cola logo and bottle have made their presence felt in hundreds of movies around the world, from smash Hollywood hits, such as *King Kong* (1933) and *Bonnie and Clyde* (1967), to art house classics, such as Japanese director Jisujiro Ozu's *Late Spring* (1949). Although in most of these movies, Coke makes only a fleeting cameo appearance, in others it plays a truly critical role.

Set during the Cold War, *One, Two, Three* (1961) is a comedy that features a Coca-Cola bottler—James Cagney—who agrees to take care of his boss's 17-year-old daughter when she visits West Berlin and has his life turned upside down when he discovers she has secretly married an East German Communist.

The Gods Must Be Crazy (1980) is set in Botswana and revolves around the discovery of a Coke bottle casually dropped in the desert from an airplane—something never seen before by Xi, a Bushman. Up to now, Xi and his relatives have been leading a contented existence because the gods have given them all they need. However, the Coke bottle, thought to be a divine gift, causes envy and anger among the tribe and Xi is sent to the "end of the earth" to return it to the gods.

Best supporting role

In the 1946 Christmas classic *It's a Wonderful Life*, James Stewart stars as the troubled George Bailey who works in a local pharmacy. The movie set features a Coca-Cola soda fountain, complete with

Above: *You've Got Mail* (1998)　　　　Above: *The Help* (2011)

Coke memorabilia, including stained-glass lampshades, a thermometer, and a tray.

In *On the Beach* (1959), based on Nevil Shute's novel, survivors of nuclear fallout following World War III, under the leadership of naval commander Gregory Peck, sail a submarine halfway around the world to investigate a mysterious Morse code signal, only to discover the devastating fact that it is caused not by a human operator, but by a Coke bottle resting on the transmitter and being bumped by a window shade flapping in the breeze.

A Coke vending machine makes a critical appearance in Stanley Kubrick's 1964 Cold War satire *Dr. Strangelove* when Group Captain Lionel Mandrake—played by Peter Sellers—orders Colonel "Bat" Guano (Keenan Wynn) to shoot the lock off the vending machine to get the change Mandrake needs for a vital phone call to the president of the United States in order to avert an all-out nuclear war. The dim Colonel Guano reluctantly complies but warns Mandrake that if Mandrake doesn't

get hold of the president, he will be answerable to The Coca-Cola Company.

In *Tarzan and the Valley of Gold* (1966), the jungle lord—played by Mike Henry—travels from Africa to Mexico to save a kidnapped child. During the scene where he is targeted by a gunman in a deserted bullfighting ring, Tarzan escapes by scaling the heights of the stadium and dislodging a 20-foot (6-meter) Coke bottle from an advertising display that rolls down into the arena and into the assassin.

In the 1976 spoof comedy *Silent Movie*, the nutty trio of Mel Brooks, Marty Feldman, and Dom DeLuise evade the goons of the evil Engulf & Devour movie corporation with the help of a Coca-Cola vending machine that fires cans of Coke like grenades.

In the comic book adventure *Superman II* (1980), the Man of Steel (Christopher Reeve) flings super villain General Zod (Terence Stamp) right through a Coca-Cola advertising sign high above the streets of Metropolis.

Coca-Cola signs

The first big Coca-Cola sign was painted on the side of a building in Cartersville, Georgia, in 1894, where it can still be seen today. By 1908, the Coca-Cola logo decorated 2.5 million square feet (233,000 square meters) of buildings across the United States. Today, to be found adorning the outside of the world's tallest bottling plant in Shatin, China, is a painted sign that covers nearly 35,521 square feet (3,300 square meters).

Above: The oldest Coca-Cola sign in the United States, originally painted on a brick wall outside the Young Brothers Pharmacy in the city of Cartersville, Georgia in 1894, is still in existence.

Something spectacular

With the introduction of neon lighting to the United States in 1923, Coca-Cola outdoor signs became more impressive. Known as spectaculars, the bold Coca-Cola signs can be seen around the world, from New York and Tokyo to Moscow and Brussels.

A neon spectacular sign was installed in Coke's hometown of Atlanta at a cost of $50,000 in 1948 and stayed in place there until 1981. In May 2003, a Coca-Cola sign made up of more than a mile of red neon and powered by more than 25,000 feet (7,600 meters) of wiring was added to the central Atlanta skyline.

Right: A neon Coke spectacular at Columbus Circle, New York.

Above: When Frank Robinson created the Coca-Cola logo in 1886, he could not have imagined that it would one day feature in dramatic illuminated spectaculars around the world. Here it features in the iconic sign in Atlanta, Georgia, the birthplace of Coca-Cola.

There has been a Coke sign in New York's Times Square since 1920. In 1969, this sign famously greeted Apollo astronauts home from their space mission with the words "Welcome back to Earth, home of Coca-Cola." In 2004, a new sign was introduced; six stories high, it features 32 high-definition video screens.

In 2003, the Coke neon spectacular was unveiled at Piccadilly Circus in London, England. Britain's largest permanent LED sign, it has special sensors that allow for the display to adjust to the weather so that when it is raining, giant rain drops appear on the sign, and on windy days it produces a rippling effect—a feature perfectly suited to Britain's erratic weather. The Piccadilly Circus sign played a part in the 2004 romantic comedy *Bridget Jones: Edge of Reason*, declaring Bridget (Renée Zellweger) and Mark Darcy (Colin Firth) to be "the real thing".

The gigantic spectacular on the main highway in central Taiwan can been seen from 1¼ miles (2 kilometers) away, while the revolving sign near the railroad station in Nagoya, Japan, towers 187 feet (57 meters) above the ground.

Located in Kings Cross, Sydney, Australia, and erected in 1974, is an iconic illuminated spectacular that is the largest billboard in the southern hemisphere. On the opposite side of the globe, the first spectacular sign to be unveiled in the Soviet Union was Coca-Cola's sign in Moscow's Pushkin Square in 1989.

Coca-Cola

THE DRINK

The iconic bottle

One of the challenges facing Coca-Cola and bottlers in the early days was copycat soft drinks riding on the back of the success of Coca-Cola. Beverages with names such as Koka-Kola, Coke-Ola, Sola Cola, Koka-Nola, and even the intriguingly titled Celery-Cola abounded. Soft drinks, including Coke and its imitators, were all bottled alike in generic, bottles with straight sides.

By the time there were nearly 1,000 bottlers producing Coca-Cola throughout the country, The Coca-Cola Company decided they needed a more individual bottle, one that was harder to copy and one that was instantly recognizable.

Above: A 1954 advertisement featuring the now iconic Coca-Cola contour bottle.

A cocoa bean inspires

Alexander Samuelson, a glass blower by trade, and Earl R. Dean from the Root Glass Company in Terre Haute, Indiana, won a contest to design a new bottle. The brief was to design a bottle so distinctive that it could be recognized even by touch in the dark and shaped in such a way that, even if it were broken, it could be identified at a glance. Taking their inspiration from an illustration of a cocoa bean with its convoluted shape and vertical grooves, Samuelson and Dean created the first prototype of the now-famous contour bottle. The unique design, described by some as the "hobble-skirt" bottle, was modified and slimmed down to work with the majority of bottling equipment and adopted in 1916.

Since then, the Coca-Cola bottle has been an inspiration for artists, including Andy Warhol, Howard Finster, Carlos Vegar, and Steve Penley. Blues players have been known to use necks from the contour bottle to play slide guitar, hence the term "bottleneck slide," and very thick eyeglasses have become known as "Coke bottle glasses."

In 1977, the United States Patent Office recognized the now-familiar bottle itself as a trademark, a designation accorded to only a handful of other packagings.

1899–1902   1900–1916

COKE IN MANY GUISES

- **Coke comes in king size** In 1955, for the first time, Coke was available in different-size bottles. There are 6½-fluid-ounce (200-milliliter), 10-fluid-ounce (300-milliliter), 12-fluid-ounce (350-milliliter), and 26-fluid-ounce (800-milliliter) bottles.

- **A can of Coke** In 1960, steel cans, first developed to make Coke more portable for armed forces overseas, were introduced to U.S. supermarkets. The 7½-fluid-ounce (220-milliliter) mini can made its first appearance in 2009.

- **Coke in space** Coca-Cola became the first soft drink in space when astronauts tested the Coca-Cola "Space Can" onboard the Space Shuttle *Challenger* in July 1985 and again on the Soviet Space Station *Mir* in 1991.

- **Recyclable bottles** In 1978, the 68-ounce (2-liter) poly-ethylene terephthalate (PET) plastic bottle was introduced and, in 2009, PlantBottle PET packaging was brought in. These plastic bottles, made partly from plant base materials, including sugar cane extracts, are completely recyclable.

- **For your refrigerator** A slim-line 12 can carton, designed to take up less refrigerator space, made its debut in 2001.

- **Available in aluminum** An aluminum contour bottle, aimed at use in nightclubs and at special events, was unveiled in 2005.

- **Limited editions** Limited edition cans and bottles have marked special events, such as the Olympic Games, the British royal wedding in 1981, and the release of *Harry Potter and the Chamber of Secrets* movie in 2002.

1915   1916   1961   1991

1994   2007   2008   2009

31

Dispensing refreshment

Innovations in design over the years have helped to make chilled Coca-Cola conveniently available almost everywhere.

In 1923, Coke introduced the six-bottle carton that made it more convenient for people to take a supply of Coke home with them (see page 14). In 1929, this was joined by another innovation—a metal open-top cooler that made it possible to serve and buy ice cold Coca-Cola. The cooler was later improved with the addition of mechanical refrigeration and automatic coin control. Now people could get Coke at service stations, stores, factories, offices, railroad stations—just about everywhere they went.

Modern technology

In 1933, the Dole Master debuted at the Chicago World's Fair. This, the first automated fountain dispenser, combined the syrup and carbonated water as the drink was poured, producing ready-to-drink Coca-Cola. Visitors to the Fair, used to seeing Coca-Cola mixed in a glass with a spoon, were amazed to see it being poured simply by pulling a handle. In 1935, the first coin-operated vending machines were used, heralding the era of self-service and making it more convenient because there didn't need to be an attendant nearby to take your money.

Above: A 1951 ad shows how far dispensing Coke had moved on from when a syrup urn was used back in the late 1800s.

Cold Coke far and wide

Popular in the 1950s were the metal—and later, plastic—coolers given away as promotional items by Coca-Cola that allowed for people to take chilled Coke on picnics, to the beach, to sporting events, camping, and on all kinds of outings.

In 1947, Raymond Loewy developed a sleek new fountain dispenser, the Dole Deluxe. Loewy was an industrial designer famous for, among other things, designing locomotives, the Studebaker Avanti and Champion model cars, and, in 1975, the interior of the Air France Concorde.

The latest dispenser, unveiled in 2009, is the Coca-Cola Freestyle Vending Machine, which lets people choose from more than 100 beverages. It eliminates the need for 30 percent of the water and packaging used along the traditional supply chain, so reducing the total carbon footprint.

Above: A summer picnic is completed with iced Coke, thanks to a picnic cooler, in this 1949 advertisement.

Above: A front view of the innovative post-mix dispenser that was launched aboard the Space Shuttle *Endeavour*.

Special delivery

Among the more unusual coolers were those developed especially for airlines so that stewardesses could serve Coke in the skies. Distinctively shaped and compact, they were designed to fit into a small space onboard the aircraft. Early versions were made of cardboard, while later versions were made of stainless steel or painted in the signature red of Coca-Cola. To dispense Coke deep under water, in 1957 a special cup-vending machine, which had to be adapted to fit through the vessel's hatch, was installed onboard the atomic submarine *Nautilus*. In 1996, an innovative Coke dispenser was launched aboard the Space Shuttle *Endeavour*.

Coca-Cola facts and figures

A 11-fluid-ounce (330-ml) can of Coke has 139 calories.

Coca-Cola has 92,800 employees worldwide.

Coca-Cola is the second most widely understood term in the world, after "okay."

Coke Zero is available in more than 100 countries around the world.

The first woman to serve on the board of a major U.S. corporation was Lettie Pate Evans, who joined the Board of Directors of The Coca-Cola Company in 1934.

Coca-Cola was first sold in England on August 31, 1900, but wasn't available to buy regularly until the early 1920s, when it was sold in London at a few places, including Selfridges on Oxford Street.

More than 1.8 billion servings of Coca-Cola are sold globally every day.

The first TV commercial for Coke was broadcast on Thanksgiving Day in 1950.

The abbreviation "Coke" was used for the first time in magazine ads in 1941.

Decades of the "nickel Coke" ended after World War II, when the price of a bottle of Coca-Cola was increased from 5 cents for the first time since 1886.

If all the Coca-Cola ever produced were to cascade down Niagara Falls at its normal rate of 1.6 million gallons (605,666 liters) per second, it would flow for nearly 83 hours.

Celebrities including Elton John, Paula Abdul, Pierce Brosnan and Duffy have appeared in ads for Diet Coke.

The Coca-Cola Facebook page, established by two fans in 2008, has more than 50 million fans to date.

Coca-Cola means "delicious happiness" in Mandarin.

The Coca-Cola Collectors' Club, whose members collect all kinds of Coke memorabilia, was formed in 1974. It now has 5,000 members in 28 countries.

The Coca-Cola Company is the world's largest beverage company.

Diet Coke was introduced to the world at a gala event at Radio City Music Hall in New York on July 8, 1982.

The Coca-Cola Company headquarters are in Atlanta, Georgia, where Dr. John Stith Pemberton first made Coca-Cola more than 125 years ago.

A black-and-white painting of a Coke bottle by Pop Art icon Andy Warhol, entitled Large Coca-Cola, sold at a Sotheby's New York auction for $35.36 million in 2010.

In 1988 three independent surveys confirmed Coca-Cola as the best-known trademark in the world.

On December 18, 1978, the day after China and the United States announced the establishment of formal diplomatic relations, Coca-Cola announced its return to the Chinese market after a 30-year absence.

Coke Zero made its debut in 2005.

DRINK

Coca-Cola

REG. U.S. PAT. OFF.

IN BOTTLES

Mighty
refreshing

Coca-Cola

THE ADS

Early advertising

Even in the early days, attention was focused on advertising and the words Coca-Cola appeared on a huge range of promotional material, including sheet music, calendars, pocket knives, trays, and bookmarks as well as in print advertisements and posters.

Below: A young nineteenth-century beauty, resplendent in feathers, holds up a glass of Coca-Cola in this 1901 advertisement. In front of her is a piece of paper that gives the location of the "Home Office [of the] Coca-Cola Co." and some of the branch offices.

Above: Regal-looking opera singer Lillian Nordica was one of the first celebrities to feature in Coca-Cola advertising.

Coca-Cola

THE GREAT NATIONAL DRINK
AT
THE GREAT NATIONAL GAME

Patrons and athletes alike find Coca-Cola as much a part of their enthusiasm as the game itself. Napoleon Lajoie, the great Cleveland batsman-manager, says: "I drink Coca-Cola regularly and have been doing so for years. It is the best, most refreshing beverage an athlete can drink." Rube Waddell says he keeps it on the bench for an emergency, and that its REFRESHING! INVIGORATING! SUSTAINING! qualities have pulled him out of many a tight place.

Above: Beginning in 1903, The Coca-Cola Company introduced advertisements featuring famous Major League baseball players in what was one of the first uses of sports endorsers in advertising. This 1907 ad has Cleveland player-manager Napoleon "Nap" Lajoie declaring "I drink Coca-Cola regularly and have been doing so for years. It is the best, most refreshing beverage an athlete can drink."

Below: In this magazine ad from 1906, a sophisticated couple share a romantic moment and a glass of Coca-Cola at the theater.

The slogans

For more than a century, Coca-Cola has used a variety of catchy slogans in its advertising that reflect not just the brand but the times. The 1906 slogan "The Great National Temperance Beverage" appealed to a society looking for an alternative to alcohol, for example, while some, such as the 1929 slogan "The Pause that Refreshes," refer to the taste of the drink.

Other slogans pick up on the social aspect of the drink, such as 1948's "Where There's Coke There's Hospitality" and "Things Go Better with Coke" in the 1960s. The "Thirst Knows No Season" slogan of the 1920s helped people to perceive Coca-Cola as something to enjoy in winter, not just summer.

Right: The slogan "Delicious and refreshing" appeared during several decades of Coke advertising, including in this 1939 poster.

HERE'S A SELECTION OF SNAPPY SLOGANS FROM OVER THE YEARS:

1886 Delicious and Refreshing

1907 Good to the Last Drop

1917 Three Million a Day

1922 Thirst Knows No Season

1927 Around the Corner from Everywhere

1932 Ice Cold Sunshine

1938 The Best Friend Thirst Ever Had

1957 Sign of Good Taste

1958 The Cold, Crisp Taste of Coke

1963 Things Go Better with Coke

1969 It's the Real Thing

1976 Coke Adds Life

1979 Have a Coke and a Smile

1982 Coke Is It!

1988 You Can't Beat the Feeling

1993 Always Coca-Cola

2001 Life Tastes Good

2005 Make It Real

2009 Open Happiness

Above, right, and below: From the first ad in 1886, Coke advertising has featured direct, simple, and memorable slogans.

41

Famous faces

In the early 1900s, Hilda Clark, a music hall performer, and Lillian Nordica, a noted opera singer and one of the first American sopranos to perform in Europe, became the first celebrities to endorse Coca-Cola. They were to be at the head of a long line of famous faces associated with Coca-Cola.

In 1934, the popular movie stars Jackie Cooper, Wallace Beery, Maurice Chevalier, Jean Harlow, and Joan Crawford all appeared in Coca-Cola advertising.

In one of the first Coke TV advertisements in the U.K., Alf Davies and Julie Reaby, winners of the 1956 British Ballroom Dancing Championship, dipped and twirled around the dance floor, accompanied by the slogan "Coca-Cola puts you at your sparkling best!"

Elvis Presley promoted Coke during his last tour in 1977. In more recent years, Coke advertisements have featured celebrities that include comic actor Bill Cosby, singer Kylie Minogue, Courtney Cox of long-running TV series *Friends* fame, Bollywood star Aishwarya Rai, and actress Penelope Cruz.

Above right: Ronan Keating, leader singer of Irish band Boyzone, in a British magazine advertisement for Diet Coke.

Right: Penelope Cruz enjoys a Coca-Cola in a 2002 advertising campaign that aimed to show that celebrities are real people, too.

Above: Actress Kim Basinger in a 2003 Diet Coke advertisement.

Singing along

Coke Time, which starred singer Eddie Fisher, began broadcasts on television and radio in 1953 and ran for four years. The program proved so popular that Coca-Cola issued promotional records of the songs featured on *Coke Time*.

In the 1960s, more than 200 popular singers and groups, including The Supremes, Ray Charles—whose version won an award for best radio commercial in 1965—Marvin Gaye, Gladys Knight and the Pips, Aretha Franklin, Lulu, Petula Clark, and Neil Diamond gave their own musical spin to the popular *Things Go Better with Coke* jingle on the radio. These commercials became hits, with listeners bombarding radio stations with requests to play them. Coke distributed 60,000 promotional *Swing the Jingles* records featuring the likes of Roy Orbison and the Drifters. The Who recorded their version of the jingle as a background to a British TV ad that featured London landmarks Carnaby Street and Piccadilly Circus.

And, of course, Coca-Cola has also made its mark in the lyrics of some huge hits, including *Come Together* by The Beatles, The Beach Boys' *All Summer Long,* and *Lola* by The Kinks.

Sports stars

Advertising spotlighting sports celebrities began with a campaign in 1905, when world champion professional bicycle racer, Jack Prince, attested that he drank only Coca-Cola while in training.

In 1934, Johnny Weismuller—swimming gold medalist in 1924 and 1928—was the first Olympian to endorse Coca-Cola. He featured on serving trays and posters alongside actress Maureen O'Sullivan, who played Jane to his Tarzan in a string of movies in the 1930s.

TV commercials in Britain in the 1950s featured, among others, renowned racing driver Stirling Moss and cricketer Alec Bedser. Other sports personalities with a Coca-Cola connection include golfer Arnold Palmer, athlete Michael Jordan, and boxing legend Muhammed Ali.

1910s and 1920s

In 1911, The Coca-Cola Company spent more than one million dollars on advertising, a vast sum of money in those days, and their efforts to make Coca-Cola a household name were unstinting. In 1913 alone, for example, they delivered one million calendars and five million metal signs to soda fountains and stores.

Above: Fashionable travelers at a railroad station soda fountain fortify themselves with Coca-Cola before their journeys in this pretty 1910 advertisement.

Left: From the very beginning, Coca-Cola has been associated with highdays and holidays. This print ad from 1916 shows a well-dressed woman enjoying a glass of Coca-Cola in front of an inviting beach scene.

Below: This advertisement, which appeared in a 1922 issue of the *Saturday Evening Post*, was part of the "Thirst Knows No Season" campaign, aimed at encouraging people to enjoy Coca-Cola all year round and not to see it just as a beverage suitable for the hot summer months.

Above: Haddon Sundblom's award-winning "Yes Girl" poster.

Bathing beauties

The Coca-Cola girl has appeared in many advertisements and in many guises over the decades, with a demure, primly attired girl on a calendar in 1891, to girls wearing uniforms and working in factories during World War II, and onward. Among the most memorable of these ads are those featuring the bathing beauties.

Many companies throughout history have used women in swimsuits to promote their brands and, for Coca-Cola, scenes featuring girls clad in swimsuits—relaxing at the beach or, in a few ads, shown energetically sailing or waterskiing—were an enduring advertising theme from

the 1920s to the 1950s. The women depicted in the swimsuit ads are "the-girl-next-door" types—attractive, smiling, athletic, and generally brunette. Men appeared occasionally but mostly in the background—perhaps holding out a towel or proffering a bottle of cold Coke.

The ads and posters from these decades are today among the most collectable of all Coke memorabilia, and none epitomizes this era more than the now-famous "Yes Girl" billboard, painted by Haddon Sundblom—who won a prestigious "Poster of the Year" award for it—which appeared in July 1946.

Above, right, and left:
A bevy of seaside beauties appear in advertisements; these—clockwise from the top—are from 1940, 1938, and 1935.

1930s and 1940s

By 1927, more Coca-Cola was being sold in bottles than at soda fountains and ads in the 1930s promoted the handy carry-home carton. Patriotic images, such as men and women in military uniform, not surprisingly dominated the advertising of the 1940s.

Above and right: A woman clad in an elegant white evening dress holds a soda-fountain glass of Coca-Cola in this image, while on the tray in front of her there are two contour bottles. Painted by Hayden Hayden, this image was used on serving trays and posters in 1936.

Above: This 1935 advertisement shows the six-bottle carry-home carton that Coca-Cola had devised and patented in 1923. It gets across the message that Coke is something to be enjoyed at home, as an accompaniment to your favorite food—in this case, sandwiches.

Above: Haddon Sundblom was the artist responsible for this heartwarming painting, *Soldier at Home*, which captures the joy of families reunited after World War Two. The slogan for the 1945 advertisement was "Christmas together ... Have a Coke ... welcome a fighting man home from the wars."

Above: "Join me," invites a women in fencing dress, as she leans against a Raymond Loewy-designed cooler, Coke bottle in hand, in this 1947 advertisement.

The artists

From the early 1900s to the 1960s, when photography took over from illustration, The Coca-Cola Company used the work of some of America's most prominent artists in its advertisements.

Norman Rockwell (1894–1978)

Much loved for his depictions of everyday life in small-town America, Norman Rockwell found commercial success early, painting his first commission when he was 15 years old. He went on to create more than 320 covers for *The Saturday Evening Post*. Between 1928 and 1935, Rockwell painted six illustrations for Coca-Cola that were used on calendars, serving trays, and posters.

Perhaps the best-known illustration is *Out Fishin'*, which depicts a young boy fishing, with his dog and a bottle of Coca-Cola for companionship. The image appeared on the 1935 Coca-Cola calendar. Coca-Cola owns three of the six illustrations and, in 2012, launched a campaign to try to find the three "lost" ones.

Right: Norman Rockwell's *Out Fishin'* was inspired by Edgar Guest's popular poem of the same name.

N. C. Wyeth (1882–1945)

One of the United States' greatest illustrators, Newell Conyers Wyeth was commissioned to illustrate a number of magazine ads, calendars, and posters for Coca-Cola, in which he captured an idyllic vision of American life. He produced the calendar for the company's fiftieth anniversary in 1936, which depicts a grizzled old fisherman taking a break from his chores, and a young girl taking a break from paddling in the sea, sharing a bottle of Coke and a quiet moment together.

Above: N. C. Wyeth's painting for Coca-Cola's fiftieth anniversary calendar.

Haddon H. Sundblom (1899–1976)

The artist, more than any other, whose work was to become synonymous with Coca-Cola is Haddon Sundblom. He trained at the Art Institute of Chicago and the American Academy of Art. For almost 40 years, he created illustrations for Coca-Cola, including many of the Coca-Cola Girls, among them the classic "Yes Girl" poster (see page 46). However, what the world remembers Sundblom for most was his depictions of Santa Claus (see pages 52–53).

Other important artists include Gil Elvgren (1914–1980), who was a student of Haddon Sundblom, and his many illustrations of Coca-Cola Girls are part of the Coca-Cola artistic heritage. Frederick Mizen (1888–1964) illustrated the first Coca-Cola billboard in 1925 and produced illustrations for newspaper and magazine advertisements. Probably his best-known painting is *Old Faithful*, a whimsical depiction of a bear in Yellowstone National Park enjoying a Coke.

Left: Haddon H. Sundblom's painting of teenagers taking a break from playing baseball for Coca-Cola's May/June 1952 calendar.

Santa Claus

Haddon Sundblom is most remembered for his enduring images of Santa Claus, which have appeared throughout the world. Sundblom helped shape our image of Santa; up until his illustrations were seen, Santa had appeared as a variety of images, even as a somewhat scary elf, but Sundblom's jovial, ruddy-cheeked, white-haired man became the Santa we all know and love.

In 1931, Sundblom was commissioned to produce images of Santa Claus, a character associated with winter, for an ad campaign aimed at encouraging people to drink Coke in cold, as well as warm, weather. He was to paint oil portraits of Santa, used in magazine advertising, store displays, billboards, posters, and calendars, for the next 33 years. These original paintings remain among the most prized possessions of The Coca-Cola Company and have been exhibited in a number of countries, including at the Louvre in Paris.

Above: Sshh … Santa tries to stop a dog from barking while he enjoys a refreshing Coca-Cola in this 1961 advertisement.

A little bit of neighborly help

Originally, Sundblom based his Santa Claus on an elderly neighbor, Lou Prentiss, and when he passed away, Sundblom used himself as a model, painting while looking in the mirror.

The adorable children who appear with Santa in some of Sundblom's paintings were based on the children living next to him; although both of them were girls, one appears as a boy in the paintings. Even the dog that appeared in the last Santa Claus painting that Sundblom created for Coca-Cola was based on a poodle owned by a neighboring florist.

Above: A 1949 Christmas advertisement depicting Santa Claus and Sprite Boy, a character who featured in Coke advertising in the 1940s and 1950s.

Fan mail

People loved Sundblom's annual Santa images and, one year, when Santa's belt was painted backward—presumably because Sundblom, using himself as a model looking in the mirror, had seen the belt in reverse—a fan wrote to point this out to Coca-Cola. Likewise, a few years later, when Santa Claus was painted without a wedding ring, there were concerned letters asking what had become of Mrs. Claus.

Above: Haddon Sundblom used himself as model to create his much-loved Santa Claus paintings.

1950s

Postwar America was affluent and mobile; the ads from this era show people of enjoying themselves at parties, at the beach, at barbecues. Whatever the occasion and wherever they were, people were shown having fun, and Coke was there, too. At the same time, Coca-Cola—and its advertising—was spreading rapidly around the globe.

Below: This painting by artist Jack Potter depicts a glamorous group seated around a coffee table in a house overlooking Diamond Head in Hawaii. In front of them is a platter of tropical fruit and bottles of Coca-Cola. It was used in the "Sign of Good Taste" advertising campaign in 1957.

Above: Commonly known as "the lady in red," this poster of a sultry woman in a beautiful red dress was created in 1950 to advertise Coca-Cola in Brazil. The very effective single-word slogan translates from Portuguese as "Incomparable."

Left: Another from the 1957 "Sign of Good Taste" campaign, this wholesome advertisement shows that all that is needed for a great party 50s-style are a roaring fire, fresh popcorn, a barrel of ice-cold Coke, and good friends. It was created from a painting by artist Bernie Fuchs.

Below: In this 1955 advertisement from the "Coke Time" and "Join the Friendly Circle" campaigns, a group of carefree young adults swim in the sea and hang onto the raft holding their precious cargo of Coke bottles chilling.

1960s

The 1960s saw a shift toward photography from the illustrations that had characterized advertising previously. At the same time, television rapidly replaced both radio and magazines as a major source of entertainment and focus of marketing for all commercial brands, including Coca-Cola. Popular music helped to deliver Coke's advertising message, with the jingle "Things Go Better with Coca-Cola" becoming a radio hit and going on to be recorded by numerous artists, including Marvin Gaye, Neil Diamond, and Roy Orbison.

Be really refreshed! Relax with Coke! Only Coca-Cola gives you the cheerful lift that's bright and lively... the cold crisp taste that deeply satisfies! No wonder Coke refreshes you best!

FOR THE PAUSE THAT REFRESHES

Above: This romantic 1960s ad illustrated that everything – even a rainy day – could be improved by a bottle of Coca-Cola and "Be really refreshed" was a major advertising slogan for the decade.

Left: This German Christmas ad depicts a happy snowman holding a pine branch and two bottles of Coke and reminds people that Coca-Cola "makes everything joyful."

For extra fun take more than one

take an extra carton of Coke.

Left: The company continued packaging innovation by introducing Coke in cans in 1960, making the drink easier than ever to transport. This 1967 advertisement, showing cans in what was known as the "Harlequin" design, promotes the new lift-top version of the can.

Below: Despite these innovations, this French advertisement from 1962, simply showing the contour bottle and a glass filled with Coca-Cola and ice with lime on the side, displays the timeless beauty of Coke's classic packaging.

1970s

Coke advertising in the 1970s was marked by possibly the most enduring of Coca-Cola's slogans, "It's the Real Thing," which was first used in 1942 and revived in 1969. A key part of the "It's the Real Thing" campaign was the now famous 1971 "Hilltop" commercial, a piece of advertising that still, several decades on, has a lasting connection with the viewing public (see page 60 for more about this ad).

Above: The result of three years of research and market testing and aimed at both the young and the young at heart, the "Coke Adds Life..." campaign was introduced in 1976.

Left: A far cry from the glamorous beauties who had dominated Coke advertising in the first half of the twentieth century, ads of the 1970s reflected the appeal of Coke in real-life situations and across all ages, genders, and ethnicities.

It's the real thing.
Coke.

The American thirst is as
independent as its spirit.
It wants real refreshment.
And during the hot steaming
summer the real refreshing taste of
Coca-Cola quenches the American
thirst better than any soft drink.
This Fourth of July, treat your thirst to the
exciting taste of Coca-Cola.
And discover why America calls it the Real Thing.

Above: Since 1886, Coca-Cola has been as much a part of the traditional American way of life as has celebrating American Independence Day on the Fourth of July.

Summer's coming.

It's the real thing.

Above: Condensation on an ice-cold can of Coke promises delicious refreshment in this 1971 magazine ad. The can features the Dynamic Ribbon Device, better known as the Coke "wave," which was launched in 1970.

I'd like to buy the world a Coke

One of the most popular ads for Coke and one of the most iconic commercials of all time, the 1971 "Hilltop" ad, as it is often called, began life when heavy fog diverted a plane bound for London to Shannon in Ireland. Bill Backer, who was creative director on the Coca-Cola account for McCann-Erickson and onboard that plane, watched passengers waiting at the airport to continue their journey getting to know each other and swapping stories about life over bottles of Coke.

The song *I'd Like to Buy the World a Coke* was written in less than 24 hours and recorded by British folk music group The New Seekers; however, producing the visual component of the ad was enormously challenging. Originally, it was to be shot on the cliffs of Dover in England, but, after three days of continuous rain, filming was moved to Rome.

Above: People from more than 20 countries around the world appeared in the *I'd Like to Buy the World* a Coke advertisement.

On an Italian hilltop

The advertisement's international cast included people from more than 20 countries lip-syncing to The New Seekers' recording on a hillside outside Rome. The lead singer was Linda Neary, a British nanny working in Italy, who was seen just two days before the shoot by producers and persuaded to take the part after the original lead singer pulled out to go on her honeymoon.

The ad was released in the United States in July 1971 and was a dramatic hit; by November, Coca-Cola had received more than 100,000 letters about the advertisement. The lyrics were adapted to remove the Coke reference, and the song was renamed *I'd Like to Teach the World to Sing* and released as a single. Since that original recording, the song has been recorded more than 75 times. Coca-Cola donated $80,000 from the sale of the song to UNICEF.

Above: More than 40 years later, the "Hilltop", as it is still consistently named, is one of the best commercials of all time.

"I'd like to buy the world a home and furnish it with love,
Grow apple trees and honey bees, and snow-white turtle doves.
I'd like to teach the world to sing in perfect harmony,
I'd like to buy the world a Coke and keep it company.
It's the real thing, Coke is what the world wants today."
(R. COOK/R. GREENWAY/B. BACKER/B. DAVIS)

1980s

The 1980s saw the hundredth anniversary of Coca-Cola and the first-ever extensions of the trademark with the introduction of Diet Coke in 1982 and caffeine-free versions of Coke and Diet Coke in 1983. Global ad campaigns were targeted at spreading the word about these new drinks.

Above: A 1983 advertisement featuring Bill Cosby, star of the 1980s hit sitcom *The Cosby Show*, one of many celebrities to endorse Coca-Cola in its long history of advertising.

Left: A simple single word, "Flavor," sums up the appeal of Diet Coke in this 1985 advertisement aimed at Hispanic-speaking Americans.

Above: This mouthwatering magazine advertisement from 1986 was part of the "Coke Is It!" campaign, which was launched in 1982.

Left: The advertising campaign had international reach; this iconic 1980s Spanish ad featuring a stylish table attendant brandishes the Spanish version of the Coke Is It! slogan: "Coca-Cola es así."

1990s

The 1990s was a time of continued growth for The Coca-Cola Company, selling one billion servings of its products every day, and advertising continued to entertain and inform. The beginning of the decade signaled the debut of the popular "Always Coca-Cola" campaign in 1993, and the world met the lovable Coke polar bear (see page 66).

Above: The "You Can't Beat the Feeling" campaign, which began in 1989 and ran throughout the 1990s, was based on the idea that nothing tops having a good time with friends, family, and, of course, Coca-Cola.

Left: First appearing in 1995, the slogan "Just for the Taste of It," emphasized that Diet Coke might be sugar free, but it was full of delicious, refreshing flavor.

Left: To highlight the link between enjoying Coke and enjoying a soccer or football match, the successful and long-running "Eat Football, Sleep Football, Drink Coca-Cola" campaign was launched in 1996, with advertising adapted to suit different countries.

Above: Part of the "Always Coca-Cola" campaign, this 1996 ad reflects Coca-Cola's longstanding association with major sporting events around the globe.

Left: "Always Coca-Cola," a catchy slogan that was first introduced in 1993, reminds people that Coke was the original and will always be the best.

The polar bears

The first time a polar bear featured in a Coca-Cola advertisement was in France in 1922. For the next 70 years, polar bears would appear occasionally in print advertisements, but in 1993 one of the most popular symbols of Coke advertising made his screen appearance—the animated polar bear in an advertisement called *Northern Lights*.

Creator Ken Stewart was inspired by his dog, which had resembled a polar bear when it was a puppy, and came up with the concept when musing over how people drink Coke while watching a movie. The ad depicts two polar bears watching the aurora borealis (which is the "movie") while they enjoy a Coke.

The polar bear series of advertisements, each only 30 seconds long, took 12 weeks each to produce and employed what were then highly innovative technical approaches, such as computer animation. Ken Stewart and a team of animators studied films and photos of polar bears to incorporate realistic movement of the bears' heads and bodies into the ads. Music was kept to a minimum to help maintain the magical air of the world of bears and the "oohs," "ahs," and grunts of bears— the only dialogue—was Ken Stewart's own voice altered by computer.

Above: A polar bear gives the sun a Coca-Cola in the first of Coke's print advertisements featuring the animal, from 1922.

The cute and mischievous polar bear has gone on to star in many Coca-Cola ads, including soaring off a ski jump in a poster for the 1994 Winter Olympics in Lillehammer, Norway. Over the years, the cuddly polar bear family has grown to include cute baby cubs, who in one hit festive season ad help the adult bear select a Christmas tree.

Above: Polar bears share a Coke and a romantic moment as they gaze at the moon in this 2002 advertisement.

2000s

Coca-Cola advertising has always reflected the constantly changing world we live in, and with the new century have come new media and technology, and innovative ways of spreading the Coke message. These include web sites, blogs, YouTube, Twitter, and Facebook—all a long way from the coupons and calendars that began a rich advertising heritage in the 1880s.

Above: This 2006 advertisement showcases some of the huge range of Coca-Cola products available around the world, including Fanta and Lilt.

Left: A poster from the 2009 "I'm No Superwoman" campaign for Diet Coke, which featured confident women taking a stand against the pressures of modern life. As part of the campaign Welsh singer Duffy appeared in a TV advertisement singing "I've Gotta To Be Me."

SERVING SUGGESTION.

Above: This 2003 ad makes subtle and effective use of the instantly recognizable shape of the iconic hobble-skirt bottle, a shape so distinctive that it was patented in 1977.

Below: Charming Tort, the tortoise, was the star of the 2005/2006 campaign of entertaining advertisements to promote Diet Coke.

DRINK Coca-Cola
REG. U.S. PAT. OFF
PAUSE REFRESH
LUNCH

Coca-Cola

THE RECIPES

French Onion Soup

**SERVES 4
(MAKES ABOUT 6 CUPS/
1.5 LITERS/2½ PINTS)**

4 tablespoons (50 g/2 oz) butter
   or margarine
3 onions, thinly sliced
2½ cups (600 ml/20 fl oz) beef stock
1⅓ cups (325 ml/11 fl oz) water
¾ cup (175 ml/6 fl oz) Coke Zero®
½ teaspoon vinegar
salt and black pepper
2 thick baguette slices per portion
½ cup (40 g/1½ oz) grated
   Parmesan cheese

Coke Zero® adds extra depth of flavor to a comforting French classic that always proves to be a winner on a chilly day.

Melt the butter in a saucepan with a heavy bottom. Add the onion and sauté until golden, but do not let the onion brown.

Add the beef stock, water, Coke Zero®, and vinegar and season with salt and black pepper to taste. Cover and let simmer for 20–25 minutes.

Meanwhile, under a preheated broiler (grill), toast one side of each of the baguette slices. Turn, generously sprinkle with the Parmesan cheese, and toast until browned.

Ladle the soup into deep bowls and top each portion with two slices of toast, cheese side up.

	CALORIES	SUGARS	FAT	SATURATED FAT	SALT
PER SERVING	438 cal (kcal)	8.8 g	15.5 g	8.8 g	2.6 g
GDA	22%	10%	22%	44%	43%

Italian Minestrone Soup

SERVES 8
(MAKES ABOUT 11½ CUPS/ 2.75 LITERS/5 PINTS)

2 bacon slices, diced
1⅔ cups (400 g/13 oz) rinsed and
    drained, canned kidney beans
½ cup (50 g/2 oz) bite-size green beans
1 large celery stick, diced
½ cup (75 g/3 oz) fresh or frozen peas
½ cup (50 g/2 oz) thinly sliced zucchini
    (courgette)
1 carrot, thinly sliced
½ onion, diced
¼ cup (15 g/½ oz) chopped flat-leaf
    parsley
1 garlic clove, very finely chopped
2 oz (50 g) elbow macaroni
⅔ cup (175 g/6 oz) tomato paste (purée)
1 cup (250 ml/8 fl oz) Coca-Cola®
1 tablespoon olive oil
1 tablespoon Worcestershire sauce
1 teaspoon dried Italian seasoning
    (or use a mix of dried basil, oregano,
    marjoram, and/or thyme)
salt and black pepper
grated Parmesan cheese, to serve
    (optional)

FOR THE STOCK
2½ lb (1.25 kg) boneless beef chuck,
    stewing steak, or shin of beef
10½ cups (2.5 liters/4 pints) water
2 teaspoons salt
1 small onion, sliced
½ cup (25 g/1 oz) celery leaves
1 bay leaf

This hearty soup provides a delicious meal in a bowl, and it freezes well, too. To save time, prepare the vegetables while the beef stock is simmering.

Put all the ingredients for the stock into a large saucepan, cover, and simmer for about 2½ hours, until the meat is tender. Strain the stock through a strainer or sieve; you should have about 8½ cups (2 liters/3½ pints). Reserve the meat.

Add ice cubes to the stock to harden the fat, then skim the fat from the stock. Finely dice the meat, discarding any fat and bones, until you have about 2 cups (275 g/9 oz). Combine the beef stock and meat in a large saucepan and place it over low heat.

Meanwhile, cook the diced bacon in a skillet or frying pan until crisp. Add the bacon with its fat, along with all the remaining ingredients, to the stock and season with salt and black pepper to taste. Cover and simmer for about 30 minutes, until the vegetables and macaroni are tender. Serve sprinkled with Parmesan cheese, if liked.

	CALORIES	SUGARS	FAT	SATURATED FAT	SALT
PER SERVING	154 cal (kcal)	11.3 g	3.4 g	0.8 g	1.6 g
GDA	8%	13%	5%	4%	27%

Cheddar and Roquefort Dip

**SERVES 6
(MAKES ABOUT 3 CUPS/
750 ML/1¼ PINTS)**

3 cups (375 g/12 oz) grated strong
    cheddar cheese
1 cup (125 g/4 oz) crumbled Roquefort
    or Stilton cheese
1 garlic clove, crushed
¾ cup (175 ml/6 fl oz) Diet Coke®
2 tablespoons (25 g/1 oz) soft
    margarine or butter, at room
    temperature
1 tablespoon grated onion
1½ teaspoons Worcestershire sauce
1 teaspoon dry mustard powder
    or mustard
a few drops of Tabasco sauce
salt, to taste

Serve this creamy dip as the centerpiece of a party platter with crisp, raw vegetables or, for more casual fare, spread on crusty bread or savory crackers.

Put the grated cheddar cheese and crumbled Roquefort cheese in a large mixing bowl. Add the garlic with ½ cup (125 ml/4 fl oz) of the Diet Coke® and all the remaining ingredients, seasoning with the salt to taste.

Beat with an electric mixer set to a low speed until blended. Gradually add the remaining Diet Coke®, beating on a high speed until the mixture is fairly smooth, light, and fluffy.

Store in a covered container in the refrigerator, preferably overnight, before serving. It will keep in the refrigerator for up to a week.

	CALORIES	SUGARS	FAT	SATURATED FAT	SALT
PER SERVING	370 cal (kcal)	0.3 g	31.9 g	20.1 g	2.1 g
GDA	18%	0%	46%	101%	35%

Coca-Cola® Marinated Steak

SERVES 4

4 sirloin or tenderloin steaks
   (about 200 g/7 oz each)

FOR THE MARINADE
scant 1 cup (200 ml/7 fl oz) Coca-Cola®
2 garlic cloves, crushed
zest and juice of 1 lemon
1 red chili, chopped
2 sprigs of flat-leaf parsley,
   coarsely chopped

Marinating steaks makes them more tender and full of flavor. Serve these steaks with steamed broccoli or roasted tomatoes for a simple but delicious meal.

Combine all the ingredients for the marinade in a bowl and use the mixture to coat the steaks. Cover the bowl with plastic wrap (clingfilm), then place in the refrigerator to marinate overnight. Remove from the refrigerator 30 minutes before cooking.

Heat a skillet or frying pan over high heat and cook each steak for 3 minutes on each side for medium. If you prefer well done, cook each side for an extra couple of minutes.

	CALORIES	SUGARS	FAT	SATURATED FAT	SALT
PER SERVING	283 cal (kcal)	2.7 g	9 g	4 g	0.4 g
GDA	14%	3%	13%	20%	7%

Chinese Pepper Steak

SERVES 6

2 tablespoons vegetable oil
1–1½ lb (500–750 g) boneless beef top
    round, top sirloin, or rump steak, cut
    into thin strips
1 garlic clove, very finely chopped
1 teaspoon salt
1 cup (250 ml/8 fl oz) beef stock
1 large green bell pepper, seeded and
    thinly sliced
3 celery sticks, thinly sliced
½ small onion, thinly sliced
¾ cup (175 ml/6 fl oz) Coca-Cola®
2 ripe tomatoes, peeled and cut into
    wedges
2½ tablespoons cornstarch (cornflour)
1 tablespoon soy sauce
steamed or boiled rice, to serve

This delicious stir-fry makes the most of simple, fresh ingredients, enhanced with a dash of Coca-Cola®. For a quick and tasty meal, you need look no farther than this!

Heat the oil in a deep skillet, frying pan, or flameproof casserole. Add the meat and brown over high heat for about 10 minutes, stirring occasionally. Add the garlic and salt toward the end of the 10 minutes cooking time, then add the stock, cover, and simmer for 15–20 minutes or until meat is tender.

Stir in the green bell pepper, celery, onion, and ½ cup (125 ml/ 4 fl oz) of the Coca-Cola®. Cover and simmer for 5 minutes. Do not overcook; the vegetables should be tender-crisp.

Add the tomato wedges and gently stir these into meat.

Blend the cornstarch (cornflour) with the remaining ¼ cup (50 ml/2 fl oz) of Coca-Cola® and the soy sauce. Stir the mixture into meat and cook for about 1 minute, until thickened, stirring lightly.

Serve over steamed or boiled rice.

	CALORIES	SUGARS	FAT	SATURATED FAT	SALT
PER SERVING	193 cal (kcal)	5.3 g	5.7 g	1.8 g	2.3 g
GDA	10%	6%	8%	9%	38%

Braised Beef Casserole

2 tablespoons oil
3 lb (1.5 kg) bottom round roast, rump
  roast, or topside or silverside steak
2 cups (400 g/13 oz) canned whole
  tomatoes and their juices
1 cup (250 ml/8 fl oz) Coca-Cola®
1 onion, finely chopped
2 celery sticks, finely chopped
2 garlic cloves, very finely chopped
3 tablespoons chopped flat-leaf parsley
1 tablespoon Italian seasoning or a mix
  of dried basil, oregano, marjoram,
  and/or thyme
1 tablespoon cornstarch (cornflour)
salt and black pepper

Coca-Cola® combined with fragrant Italian herbs give a unique flavor to the sauce that accompanies this succulent pot roast.

Heat the oil in a large, deep skillet, frying pan, or flameproof casserole set over medium heat, then cook the meat for about 10 minutes on each side, until browned. Drain off the fat.

Add the tomatoes and their juices to a medium-size bowl and break them up with a spoon. Add all the remaining ingredients except for the cornstarch (cornflour), season with the salt and black pepper to taste, and stir to mix well.

Pour the Coca-Cola® mixture over the meat, cover, and simmer slowly for about 2½ hours or until the meat is tender.

Remove the meat and let rest for a few minutes while you thicken the sauce. Mix the cornstarch with a little water in a small bowl until smooth, then slowly stir into the pan and heat for a few minutes until you have a thick sauce.

Slice the meat, spoon the meat over the top, and serve.

	CALORIES	SUGARS	FAT	SATURATED FAT	SALT
PER SERVING	286 cal (kcal)	5.6 g	8 g	2.4 g	0.4 g
GDA	14%	6%	11%	12%	7%

Warming Winter Goulash

SERVES 8

4 tablespoons (50 g/2 oz) butter
3 lb (1.5 kg) lean, boneless beef chuck, beef round, or stewing steak, cut into 1-inch (2.5-cm) cubes
2 onions, chopped
1 garlic clove, very finely chopped
1 tablespoon paprika
2½ teaspoons salt
½ teaspoon caraway seeds
½ cup (125 ml/4 fl oz) Coca-Cola®
¼ cup (50 ml/2 fl oz) dry red wine
4 ripe tomatoes, peeled and chopped
3 tablespoons (25 g/1 oz) all-purpose (plain) flour
freshly cooked medium egg noodles, to serve
3 tablespoons chopped flat-leaf parsley, to garnish

Ideal for feeding a hungry crowd, this satisfying beef goulash can be made ahead of time and reheated at the last minute for effortless entertaining.

Melt the butter in a large, deep skillet or frying pan and add the meat, stirring to brown the cubes on all sides. Remove the meat cubes as they brown and set aside to drain on kitchen paper towels.

Add the onion and garlic to the pan and sauté until they are softened. Stir in the paprika, salt, and caraway seeds and cook for 1 minute.

Return the meat to the pan and add the Coca-Cola®, wine, and chopped tomatoes. Cover tightly and simmer for about 1¼ hours or until the meat is tender.

Blend the flour with a little water in a small bowl to make a smooth paste, then stir it into the goulash. Cook, stirring, for 3–5 minutes, until the gravy is thickened. Serve with freshly cooked egg noodles and garnish with chopped parsley.

	CALORIES	SUGARS	FAT	SATURATED FAT	SALT
PER SERVING	322 cal (kcal)	4.9 g	12.1 g	6 g	2 g
GDA	16%	5%	17%	30%	33%

Glazed Pork Chops

SERVES 4

1 tablespoon olive oil
1 garlic clove, chopped
the leaves from 3 sprigs of thyme
2 bay leaves
3 tablespoons balsamic vinegar
1 cup (250 ml/8 fl oz) Coke Zero®
4 pork loin chops (about 5–6 oz/
  150 g each)
steamed or boiled vegetables, to serve

These tempting pork chops coated with a deliciously sticky glaze are sure to be a hit with all the family.

Heat the oil in a saucepan and gently sauté the garlic, thyme, and bay leaves for 1 minute. Add the balsamic vinegar and Coke Zero®. Bring to a boil and simmer for 10 minutes, until the sauce is nicely thickened.

Heat a ridged grill pan or griddle over medium heat and brush the chops with the glaze. Cook the chops for 5 minutes on each side or until cooked through.

Serve with cooked vegetables.

	CALORIES	SUGARS	FAT	SATURATED FAT	SALT
PER SERVING	396 cal (kcal)	0 g	31 g	10.7 g	0.2 g
GDA	20%	0%	44%	54%	3%

Coca-Cola® Ham

SERVES 10

4-lb (2-kg) smoked cured ham
    or smoked gammon
a handful of whole cloves
1 cup firmly packed (200 g/7 oz)
    brown or mucovado sugar
6½ cups (1.5 litres/2½ pints) Coca-Cola®

TO SERVE
mashed potatoes
steamed green beans

Inspired by the recipes of the American Deep South, this baked dish is infused with appetizing sweetness from Coca-Cola®.

Boil the meat for 1 hour, then remove it from the saucepan and let cool a little so you can remove the skin. Using a sharp knife, score the flesh in a diamond pattern or at intervals all the way through to the meat, then push the whole cloves into the scored areas.

Place the meat in a roasting pan or tin, then coat with one-quarter of the sugar, patting it into place. Pour the Coca-Cola® into the pan slowly, pouring some of it over the meat and sugar. (Some of the sugar will wash off into the pan.) Add the remaining sugar, patting it around the meat.

Bake in a preheated oven, at 475°F (240°C/Gas Mark 9), for 20 minutes, then reduce the heat to 375°F (190°C/Gas Mark 5) and cook for 1 hour more.

Let cool, then remove the cloves, and slice to serve. Serve with mashed potatoes and steamed green beans.

	CALORIES	SUGARS	FAT	SATURATED FAT	SALT
PER SERVING	344 cal (kcal)	17.2 g	15 g	5 g	4.5 g
GDA	17%	19%	21%	25%	75%

Coca-Cola® Chicken Wings

SERVES 8

1 cup firmly packed (200 g/7 oz) brown or muscovado sugar
1 (12-oz/330-ml) can Coke Zero®
2 onions, chopped
2 garlic cloves, very finely chopped
2 tablespoons soy sauce
2–3 lb (1–1.5 kg) chicken wings
1 tablespoon cornstarch (cornflour) (optional)
3–4 tablespoons water (optional)
salt and black pepper

These Chinese-style chicken wings with a Coke Zero® twist are perfect served with plain rice or noodles.

Combine the sugar, Coke Zero®, onion, garlic, soy sauce, and salt and pepper to taste into a large flameproof casserole.

Place the chicken wings in the sauce, turning to coat well. Put the casserole into a preheated oven, at 350°C (180°C/Gas Mark 4), for 2 hours, until the chicken is fully cooked and the juices run clear when pierced with the tip of a sharp knife or skewer.

If you prefer a thick sauce, mix the cornstarch (cornflour) with the water in a small bowl until smooth with no lumps. Put the casserole on the stove (hob) over low heat, stir in the cornstarch mixture, and simmer for a few minutes until the sauce is thickened.

	CALORIES	SUGARS	FAT	SATURATED FAT	SALT
PER SERVING	482 cal (kcal)	26.4 g	23.4 g	6.6 g	1 g
GDA	24%	29%	33%	33%	17%

Chicken Curry

SERVES 6

2½-lb (1.25-kg) chicken, rinsed
2–3 leafy celery tops
3 tablespoons (40 g/1½ oz) butter
    or margarine
1 tart apple, peeled and diced
1 onion, thinly sliced
1 tablespoon curry powder (or to taste)
⅓ cup (50 g/2 oz) raisins
½ cup (125 ml/4 fl oz) Diet Coke®
3 tablespoons (25 g/1 oz) all-purpose
    (plain) flour
1 cup (250 ml/8 fl oz) canned
    coconut milk
salt and white pepper

TO SERVE

freshly cooked basmati or other
    long-grain rice
grated coconut, chopped peanuts,
    chopped onion, raisins, or chopped
    fresh cilantro (coriander), for
    sprinkling on top of each serving
chutney, corn relish, and/or lime
    wedges

This dish is best made the day before to allow for the flavors to develop.

Put the chicken into a large saucepan of salted boiling water with the celery tops. Cover and simmer for 1 hour or until the meat is tender and the juices run clear when pierced in the thickest part with a sharp knife or skewer. Drain through a strainer or sieve, reserving the strained stock. Remove the meat from the bones and cut so you have 3 cups (375 g/12 oz) of ½-inch (1-cm) pieces (use the leftovers for a stock).

Melt the butter in skillet or frying pan. Add the apple, onion, and curry powder and sauté for 5 minutes. Stir in the raisins, 1 cup (250 ml/8 fl oz) of the reserved stock, and the Diet Coke®.

Mix the flour with the coconut milk a little at a time, stirring until smooth. Add this mixture to the onion-and-apple mixture and season with salt and white pepper to taste. Stir and cook over low heat until thick and creamy. Add the cooked chicken meat and transfer to a covered container. Chill in the refrigerator overnight.

Reheat slowly in a large saucepan until heated through. Serve with freshly cooked basmati rice and a selection of garnishes.

	CALORIES	SUGARS	FAT	SATURATED FAT	SALT
PER SERVING	344 cal (kcal)	12.5 g	8.2 g	4.2 g	0.6 g
GDA	17%	14%	12%	21%	10%

Teriyaki Chicken

SERVES 4

1 lb (500 g) boneless, skinless chicken
   breasts, cut into strips, or chicken
   wings, trimmed
vegetable oil, for greasing

FOR THE TERIYAKI MARINADE
¾ cup (175 ml/6 fl oz) soy sauce
½ cup (125 ml/4 fl oz) Coca-Cola®
2 tablespoons orange juice
1 inch (2.50cm) piece of fresh ginger
   root, peeled and very finely chopped
1 garlic clove, very finely chopped
crisp green salad, to serve
black pepper, and chili powder, to taste

This dish is sure to be a favorite for those extra-busy days because all the preparation is done the night before. It's great served with a simple, crisp green salad.

Combine all the marinade ingredients in a bowl, add the chicken, and turn to coat, then cover, and marinate overnight in the refrigerator.

Place the chicken in a well-greased roasting pan or tin, reserving the marinade. Bake the chicken in a preheated oven, at 350°F (180°C/Gas Mark 4), for about 30 minutes.

Remove the roasting pan from the oven, move the chicken around in the pan to soak up the marinade, baste with additional marinade, and return to oven for another 15 minutes, until the chicken is cooked through and the juices run clear when the thickest part of the meat is pierced with the tip of a sharp knife or skewer.

	CALORIES	SUGARS	FAT	SATURATED FAT	SALT
PER SERVING	169 cal (kcal)	6.9 g	1.4 g	0.4 g	8.1 g
GDA	8%	8%	2%	2%	135%

Salmon with Noodles

SERVES 4

2 tablespoons peanut (groundnut) oil
2-inch (5-cm) piece of fresh ginger
    root, peeled and chopped
1 garlic clove, chopped
1 red chili
¼ cup (50 ml/2 fl oz) soy sauce
1 tablespoon rice wine vinegar
scant ½ cup (100 ml/3½ fl oz)
    Coke Zero®
grated zest of 1 lime
2 salmon fillets (about 5–6 oz/
    150–175 g each)
2 cups (150 g/5 oz) finely sliced
    snow peas (mangetout)
10 oz (300 g) prepared, straight-to-
    wok egg noodles
lime wedge, to serve

This Asian-style fish dish is bursting with exotic flavors and, as a bonus, it's low in fat, too.

Heat 1 tablespoon of the oil in a small saucepan, add the ginger, garlic, and red chili, and cook for 1 minute. Pour in the soy sauce, rice wine vinegar, Coke Zero®, and lime zest and bring to a boil. Let the mixture simmer for 5 minutes, then remove from the heat and let cool completely.

Once cool, add the salmon fillets and let marinate in the refrigerator for at least 30 minutes.

Preheat the broiler or grill to medium-high. Remove the salmon from the marinade (reserving the marinade) and cook the salmon for 7 minutes on each side, brushing with the reserved marinade when you turn it.

Remove the salmon and flake the flesh using 2 forks. Heat the remaining oil in a wok and stir-fry the snow peas (mangetout) and egg noodles for 3 minutes, stir through the salmon, and serve with lime wedges.

	CALORIES	SUGARS	FAT	SATURATED FAT	SALT
PER SERVING	521 cal (kcal)	3.7 g	21.4 g	4.5 g	2.7 g
GDA	26%	4%	31%	22%	45%

Coca-Cola® Chili Tuna

SERVES 4

grated zest and juice of 1 lime
scant 1 cup (200 ml/7 fl oz) Coca-Cola®
1 green chili, seeded and chopped
1 tablespoon coriander seeds, lightly
    crushed
1 tablespoon grated fresh ginger root
4 tuna steaks about 4 oz/125 g each)
1 tablespoon olive oil

TO SERVE
stir-fried broccoli
boiled new potatoes

Tuna is an excellent source of heart-healthy omega-3 oils. Serve these steaks with stir-fried broccoli and boiled new potatoes.

Place the lime zest and juice, Coca-Cola®, chili, coriander seeds, and ginger in a bowl and mix until well combined. Add the tuna steaks, cover with plastic wrap (clingfilm), put in the refrigerator, and marinate for 30 minutes.

Heat the oil in a saucepan set over medium-high heat and cook the fish for 2 minutes on each side, until it is cooked through.

	CALORIES	SUGARS	FAT	SATURATED FAT	SALT
PER SERVING	218 cal (kcal)	5.3 g	8.7 g	1.9 g	0.2 g
GDA	11%	6%	12%	10%	3%

Mushroom Stir-fry

SERVES 4

1 tablespoon peanut (groundnut) oil
1 onion, finely sliced
1 red chili, finely sliced
1 red bell pepper, finely sliced
3½ cups (250 g/8 oz) finely sliced
   mushrooms
1⅔ cups (100 g/3½ oz) snow peas
   (mangetout)
1 garlic clove
5 oz (150 g) prepared, straight-to-wok
   rice noodles
2 tablespoons soy sauce
⅔ cup (150 ml/5 fl oz) Diet Coke®
juice of ½ lime
2 tablespoons chopped fresh cilantro
   (coriander)

Light yet satisfying, this superspeedy vegetable stir-fry is the ideal fuss-free meal when you're pushed for time.

Heat the oil in a large wok, skillet, or frying pan, add the onion, chili, and red bell pepper, and cook for 3 minutes, stirring frequently. Add the mushrooms, snow peas (mangetout) and garlic, and cook for another 2–3 minutes.

Add the noodles, soy sauce, and Diet Coke®, and cook for 1 minute, until the noodles are warmed through and the sauce has a nice thick consistency.

Stir through the lime juice and cilantro (coriander) and serve immediately with lime wedges.

	CALORIES	SUGARS	FAT	SATURATED FAT	SALT
PER SERVING	196 cal (kcal)	6.2 g	6 g	1.4 g	1.5 g
GDA	10%	7%	9%	7%	25%

Mixed Bean Chili

SERVES 4

1 tablespoon sunflower oil
1 onion, diced
2 garlic cloves, crushed
2 teaspoons ground cumin
1 teaspoon smoked paprika
1⅔ cups (400 g/13 oz) canned
    tomatoes
scant 1 cup (200 ml/7 fl oz) Coca-Cola®
3½ cups (800 g/26 oz) canned mixed
    beans, such as red kidney beans,
    pinto beans, and black beans

TO SERVE
plain rice
guacamole
sour cream
fresh cilantro (coriander)

Top this tasty vegetarian chili with guacamole, sour cream and fresh cilantro and enjoy a warming bowl of pure deliciousness.

Heat the oil in a large saucepan, add the diced onion, and sauté for 5–7 minutes, until softened. Add the garlic, cumin, and paprika and cook for another 2 minutes.

Pour in the canned tomatoes and Coca-Cola® and let the mixture simmer for 20 minutes. Stir in the mixed beans and heat until they are warmed through.

	CALORIES	SUGARS	FAT	SATURATED FAT	SALT
PER SERVING	230 cal (kcal)	11.6 g	4.1 g	0.5 g	2.2 g
GDA	12%	13%	6%	2%	37%

Goat Cheese and Bacon Salad with Coca-Cola® Vinaigrette

SERVES 4

6 smoked bacon slices
2 (about 4 oz/110 g) goat cheese logs,
   sliced into ½-inch (1-cm) thick disks
12 cherry tomatoes, halved
3½ cups (100 g/3½ oz) mixed lettuce
½ cup (50 g/2 oz) coarsely snapped
   walnut halves

FOR THE DRESSING
¼ cup (50 ml/2 fl oz) Diet Coke®
1 shallot, diced
1 tablespoon olive oil
2 teaspoons balsamic vinegar
1 teaspoon Dijon mustard

Easy to prepare, this dish is made of a mouthwatering combination of bacon, goat cheese, and crisp lettuce, offset by an unusual Diet Coke®-base dressing.

Combine the dressing ingredients in a small bowl and set aside while you prepare the salad.

Preheat the broiler (grill) to high and cook the bacon for about 4 minutes on each side, until nice and crispy. Set aside. Broil the goat cheese and tomatoes for 5 minutes.

Wash the lettuce and arrange it on plates, then top with disks of goat cheese, some bacon, and halved cherry tomatoes. Sprinkle with walnuts and drizzle with the dressing. Serve immediately.

	CALORIES	SUGARS	FAT	SATURATED FAT	SALT
PER SERVING	179 cal (kcal)	1.7 g	16.5 g	3.5 g	0.7 g
GDA	9%	2%	24%	18%	12%

Luxury Baked Beans

SERVES 6

scant 1 cup (200 ml/7 fl oz) tomato
    puree or sauce (passata)
1 tablespoon Dijon mustard
1½ tablespoons red wine vinegar
scant 1 cup (200 ml/7 fl oz) Coke Zero®
3½ cups (26 oz) canned navy
    (haricot) beans
salt and black pepper

TO SERVE
green salad
baked potatoes

Homemade baked beans are budget friendly and easy to make. Adding Coke Zero® gives them a little something extra.

Place the tomato puree (passata), mustard, vinegar, and Coke Zero® in a large bowl and whisk together until thoroughly combined. Season with salt and black pepper, then stir in the beans.

Pour the mixture into a baking dish and cook in a preheated oven, at 400°F (200°C/Gas Mark 6), for 30 minutes. Stir the contents of the baking dish and return to the oven for another 15 minutes. Serve warm.

	CALORIES	SUGARS	FAT	SATURATED FAT	SALT
PER SERVING	160 cal (kcal)	2.4 g	2.7 g	0.7 g	0.5 g
GDA	8%	3%	4%	4%	8%

Roasted Coca-Cola® Beets

SERVES 4

6 beets (beetroot)
5 sprigs of thyme
1 teaspoon cumin seeds
4 garlic cloves, crushed
1 tablespoon red wine vinegar
scant ½ cup (100 ml/3½ fl oz)
   Coca-Cola®

TO SERVE
cooked couscous
lightly toasted pumpkin seeds

Roasted beets have a sweet, mellow flavor that is enhanced by a splash of Coke®. Serve these beets stirred through couscous or alongside roasted chicken.

Peel and quarter each beet (beetroot) and place the quarters in a roasting pan with all the other ingredients. Cover with kitchen foil. Roast in a preheated oven, at 400°F (200°C/ Gas Mark 6), for 45 minutes, until tender.

To serve, toss the beets through cooked couscous and sprinkle with lightly toasted pumpkin seeds.

	CALORIES	SUGARS	FAT	SATURATED FAT	SALT
PER SERVING	91 cal (kcal)	16.7 g	0.4 g	0 g	0.4 g
GDA	5%	19%	1%	0%	7%

Caramelized Onions

SERVES 2

meat juices (from a piece of meat
  you have fried or roasted)
2 white onions, sliced
2 tablespoons Coca-Cola®

These delicious onions are great for serving alongside a juicy steak, for topping burgers, or for adding some sizzle to sausages.

Heat the meat juices in a saucepan over high heat, add the onion, and stir slightly. Add the Coca-Cola® and stir constantly for about 2–3 minutes, until the pan is deglazed and the onions are opaque.

Remove the onion from the pan and serve immediately.

	CALORIES	SUGARS	FAT	SATURATED FAT	SALT
PER SERVING	158 cal (kcal)	9.1 g	11.3 g	1.6 g	0 g
GDA	8%	10%	16%	8%	0%

Thick Barbecue Sauce

MAKES 2 CUPS (475 ML/ 16 FL OZ)

2 onions, very finely chopped
¾ cup (175 ml/6 fl oz) Coca-Cola®
¾ cup (200 g/7 oz) tomato ketchup
2 tablespoons vinegar
2 tablespoons Worcestershire sauce
½ teaspoon chili powder
salt

Once you've tried this simple, spicy homemade sauce, there'll be no going back to the store-bought variety! This is the ideal barbecue sauce to spoon over cooked burgers.

Combine all the ingredients in a saucepan, seasoning with salt to taste. Bring to a boil, then cover the pan, and reduce the heat. Simmer, stirring occasionally, for about 45 minutes until the sauce is very thick.

	CALORIES	SUGARS	FAT	SATURATED FAT	SALT
PER SERVING	88 cal (kcal)	17.8 g	0.3 g	0 g	2.7 g
GDA	4%	20%	0%	0%	45%

Cherry Coke® Cupcakes

MAKES 12 CUPCAKES

1⅔ cups (200 g/7 oz) all-purpose (plain) flour
3 tablespoons (15 g/½ oz) unsweetened cocoa powder
1½ teaspoons baking powder
¼ teaspoon baking soda (bicarbonate of soda)
¾ teaspoon salt
⅔ cup (125 g/4 oz) superfine (caster) or granulated sugar
2 eggs, lightly beaten
⅔ cup (150 ml/5 fl oz) Cherry Coke®
1 stick (125 g/4 oz) butter, melted

FOR THE FROSTING
1 stick (125 g/4 oz) butter, softened
¾ cup (100 g/3½ oz) confectioners' (icing) sugar, sifted
½ cup (100 g/3½ oz) reduced-fat crème fraîche or plain (natural) yogurt
1–2 drops of red food coloring
¼ cup (50 ml/2 fl oz) boiling water
12 fresh red cherries or 2–3 teaspoons popping candy, to decorate (optional)

The froth of pink frosting is the perfect foil for beautiful red cherries.

Sift the flour, cocoa, baking powder, baking soda (bicarbonate of soda), and salt into a large bowl and stir in the sugar. Make a well in the center of the dry ingredients, add the eggs and Cherry Coke®, and beat together using an electric mixer. Add the melted butter and beat until smooth.

Spoon the batter into 12 paper liners set in a muffin pan or tin and bake in a preheated oven, at 375°F (190°C/Gas Mark 5), for 20–25 minutes, until they are risen and firm. Transfer to a wire rack to cool.

To make the frosting, beat together the butter, confectioners' (icing) sugar, and crème fraîche until well blended. Beat in a drop or two of food coloring until a pale pink, then add boiling water, a tablespoon at a time, until the mixture comes together in a light, glossy frosting.

Spoon the frosting onto the cupcakes, shaping into a peak with the back of the spoon, or put into a pastry (piping) bag and pipe it over the cupcakes. Top each cake with a cherry or sprinkle with popping candy, if liked, and serve immediately.

	CALORIES	SUGARS	FAT	SATURATED FAT	SALT
PER SERVING	246 cal (kcal)	21.5 g	11.2 g	6.7 g	0.8 g
GDA	12%	24%	16%	34%	13%

Banana Loaf

SERVES 8–10

scant 1 stick (110 g/3¾ oz) butter, softened
1 cup firmly packed (200 g/7 oz) soft dark brown sugar
2 eggs, beaten
2¼ cups (285 g/9½ oz) all-purpose flour
2¾ teaspoons baking powder
¼ teaspoon ground cinnamon
4 medium overripe bananas, mashed
scant ½ cup (100 ml/3½ fl oz) Diet Coke®

This delicious banana loaf is a simple recipe that gives perfect results every time. It's also a great way to use up overripe fruit.

Preheat the oven to 350°F (180°C/Gas Mark 4. Lightly grease and line the bottom of a 9 x 5 x 3-inch (24 x 13 x 7-cm) loaf pan.

Cream together the butter and sugar in a large bowl, then gradually beat in the eggs, a little at a time.

Sift in the flour, baking powder, and ground cinnamon, then fold in with the mashed bananas and Diet Coke®.

Spoon the batter into the prepared loaf pan and bake for 1 hour, or until a toothpick or cocktail stick inserted in the middle of the cake comes out clean.

Turn out onto a wire rack to cool.

	CALORIES	SUGARS	FAT	SATURATED FAT	SALT
PER SERVING	296 cal (kcal)	27.9 g	10.9 g	6.2 g	0.3 g
GDA	15%	31%	16%	32%	5%

Iced Frappé Mocha

**SERVES 4
(MAKES 5 CUPS/
1.2 LITERS/2 PINTS)**

2 oz (50 g) semisweet (plain) chocolate
¼ cup (50 g/2 oz) superfine (caster) or
 granulated sugar
1 cup (250 ml/8 fl oz) double-strength
 hot coffee
2½ cups (600 ml/20 fl oz) milk
1½ cups (350 ml/12 fl oz) Coke Zero®,
 chilled
whipped cream or ice cream, to serve

Whether served as a drink or a dessert, this delectable concoction makes a grand finale to any meal. It will keep in the refrigerator for several days.

Melt the chocolate in a heatproof bowl set over a saucepan of simmering water, making sure that the bottom of the bowl does not touch the water below.

Stir in the sugar, then gradually stir in the hot coffee, mixing thoroughly. Add the milk and continue heating for about 10 minutes, until the chocolate is fully dissolved and the mixture is smooth. Let cool slightly, then pour into a heatproof jar. Cover and chill in the refrigerator.

When ready to serve, stir in the chilled Coke Zero®. Serve over ice cubes in tall glasses, topped with whipped cream as a drink, or with a scoop of vanilla ice cream as a dessert.

	CALORIES	SUGARS	FAT	SATURATED FAT	SALT
PER SERVING	213 cal (kcal)	26.4 g	9.3 g	5.9 g	0.2 g
GDA	11%	29%	13%	30%	3%

Lime Soufflé Pie

MAKES A 9-INCH (23-CM) PIE SERVING 6–8

½ envelope unflavored gelatin, or 2 unflavored gelatin leaves soaked in water for 5 minutes
⅔ cup (150 ml/¼ pint) Coke Zero®
1 cup (100 g/3½ oz) superfine (caster) or granulated sugar
2 eggs, separated
grated zest and juice of 2 limes
¼ cup (50 ml/2 fl oz) fresh lime juice
1 cup (250 ml/8 fl oz) heavy (double) cream
1 (9-inch/23-cm) store-bought baked sweet pastry shell (case)
2 tablespoons grated lime zest

Light and tangy, this chilled pie is the perfect dessert to serve at the end of a special-occasion summer dinner.

Place the gelatin, Coke Zero® and half the sugar in a small pan and gently heat to dissolve the sugar and gelatin.

Beat the egg yolks in a bowl, then stir into the Coke Zero® mixture. Continue to cook, stirring, until the mixture has thickened slightly. Remove from the heat, stir in the lime juice, then pour into a bowl and place in the fridge to cool.

Beat the egg whites in a clean bowl until they form soft peaks. Gradually beat in the remaining sugar, beating until stiff and glossy.

Whisk the heavy (double) cream with the lime zest to form really soft peaks. Gently fold this into the egg whites and then fold in the Coke Zero® mixture until it is all incorporated and smooth.

Pour into the prepared pastry shell (case) and chill in the fridge for at least 2 hours before eating. Serve decorated with lime zest.

	CALORIES	SUGARS	FAT	SATURATED FAT	SALT
PER SERVING	301 cal (kcal)	16.5 g	22.5 g	11.7 g	0.2 g
GDA	15%	18%	32%	58%	3%

Glory Muffins

MAKES 12 MUFFINS

1 cup (100 g/3½ oz) rolled (porridge) oats, finely ground
½ cup (65 g/2½ oz) wholewheat (wholemeal) flour
1⅓ cups (165 g/5½ oz) all-purpose flour
2¼ teaspoons baking powder
3 eggs
scant 1½ cup (175 g/6 oz) superfine (caster) or granulated sugar
½ cup (125 g/4 oz) unsweetened applesauce (apple puree)
2 tablespoons canola (rapeseed) oil
scant ½ cup (100 ml/3½ fl oz) Coca-Cola®
½ teaspoon vanilla extract
½ cup (65 g/2½ oz) finely grated carrots
scant ½ cup (50 g/2 oz) finely grated zucchini (courgette)
½ cup (75 g/3 oz) raisins

These delicious muffins are packed full of healthy oats, fruit, and vegetables. Easily portable, they are great for snacking on the go!

Line the holes of a muffin pan with 12 paper muffin liners.

Mix together the oats and both flours in a large mixing bowl.

In a separate bowl, whisk together the eggs, sugar, applesauce (apple puree), oil, Coca-Cola®, and vanilla extract. Gently fold the wet ingredients into the dry ingredients. Now fold in the grated carrots, grated zucchini (courgette), and raisins, until just combined, being careful not to overmix.

Spoon the batter into the prepared paper muffin liners and bake in a preheated oven, at 350°F (180°C/Gas Mark 4), for 20 minutes, until risen and golden brown. Serve warm or let cool on a wire rack.

	CALORIES	SUGARS	FAT	SATURATED FAT	SALT
PER SERVING	211 cal (kcal)	37.8 g	4.3 g	0.7 g	0.3 g
GDA	11%	16%	6%	4%	5%

Scottish Oaten Bread

MAKES A 9 × 5 × 3-INCH (24 × 13 × 7-CM) LOAF, SERVING 8

25 pitted dried prunes (about 8 oz/ 250 g), plus extra, halved, to decorate
2 cups (250 g/8 oz) all-purpose (plain) flour
½ cup (100 g/3½ oz) superfine (caster) or granulated sugar
2½ teaspoons baking powder
½ teaspoon baking soda (bicarbonate of soda)
1 teaspoon salt
1 cup (100 g/3½ oz) rolled (porridge) oats
1 egg
3 tablespoons vegetable oil or melted vegetable shortening (fat)
½ teaspoon vanilla extract
1 cup (8 fl oz/250 ml) Coca-Cola®
½ cup (50 g/2 oz) chopped walnuts

This moist, fruity bread is delicious as is or toasted and spread with cream cheese or a little butter.

Put the prunes in a heatproof bowl, cover with hot water, and let soak for about 1 hour. Drain well and chop, then set aside.

Sift the flour, sugar, baking powder, baking soda (bicarbonate of soda), and salt into a large bowl, add the oats, and mix.

Beat together the egg with the oil and vanilla extract in a small bowl until well blended, then stir this into the flour mixture. Add the Coca-Cola®, chopped prunes, and nuts, and blend thoroughly with a spoon.

Transfer the batter into a well-greased and lightly floured 9 × 5 × 3-inch (24 × 13 × 7-cm) loaf pan. If desired, decorate the top with prune halves.

Bake in a preheated oven, at 350°F (180°C/Gas Mark 4), for about 1 hour or until a toothpick or cocktail stick inserted into the center of the bread comes out clean. Let cool on a wire rack for 20 minutes before removing the loaf from the pan. Store wrapped in kitchen foil overnight before slicing.

	CALORIES	SUGARS	FAT	SATURATED FAT	SALT
PER SERVING	324 cal (kcal)	21.4 g	10.6 g	1.4 g	0.4 g
GDA	16%	24%	15%	7%	7%

Diet Coke® Crepes

SERVES 6

FOR THE CREPES
scant 1 cup (110 g/3¾ oz) all-purpose
   (plain) flour
a pinch of salt
2 eggs
scant 1 cup (200 ml/7 fl oz) milk
⅓ cup (75 ml/3 fl oz) Diet Coke®
4 tablespoons (50 g/2 oz) butter,
   for cooking

FOR THE SYRUP
scant 1 cup (200 ml/7 fl oz) Diet Coke®
grated zest of ½ lemon

TO SERVE
a selection of fresh fruit or berries
Greek yogurt or crème fraîche

Adding Coke® to the batter makes these crepes extra fluffy and light. Served with fresh fruit, they make a great Sunday brunch treat.

Sift the flour into a bowl with the salt. Make a well in the middle and crack in the eggs. Beat the eggs using a whisk, then gradually incorporate the flour from around the edges of the well. Combine the milk and Diet Coke®, and when the batter is starting to look thick, add a little of the milk mixture to the well. Keep going with this process until you have whisked in all the milk mixture and you have a nice smooth batter. Cover and let sit in the refrigerator for 30 minutes.

For the syrup, place the Diet Coke® in a pan and simmer for 8–10 minutes, until you have a glossy syrup; be careful, because it can quickly evaporate. Mix in the lemon zest.

To cook the crepes, put a small skillet or frying pan on the stove (hob) and melt a small piece of butter. Ladle in some batter and swirl it around the pan. Cook for 2 minutes or until lightly golden, then turn and cook the other side for 1–2 minutes, until golden. Repeat until all the batter has been used.

Top with fruit and yogurt, drizzle with the syrup, and serve.

	CALORIES	SUGARS	FAT	SATURATED FAT	SALT
PER SERVING	171 cal (kcal)	1.7 g	10.2 g	5.7 g	0.2 g
GDA	9%	2%	15%	28%	3%

Grenadini

SERVES 1

ice cubes
½ cup (125 ml/4 fl oz) Coke Zero®
2 tablespoons (25 ml/1 fl oz) grenadine
maraschino cherry, to decorate

The Grenadini is also sometimes called a Roy Rogers, named after the famous American singer and cowboy actor.

Fill a highball glass with ice cubes. Add the Coke Zero® and grenadine. Stir well with a long-handled spoon, decorate with the maraschino cherry, and serve with a long straw, if desired.

	CALORIES	SUGARS	FAT	SATURATED FAT	SALT
PER SERVING	91 cal (kcal)	9 g	0 g	0 g	0 g
GDA	5%	10%	0%	0%	0%

Mint Cooler

SERVES 1

5 mint sprigs
1 lime wedge
3–4 ice cubes
1 cup (250 ml/8 fl oz) Diet Coke®
mint sprig and lime wedge, to decorate

Fragrant with tangy lime and fresh mint, this drink is the perfect refresher for a hot summer day.

Muddle the mint sprigs and lime wedge at the bottom of a highball glass with a muddler or long-handled spoon. Add the ice cubes to the glass and pour the Diet Coke® over the ice. Decorate with a mint sprig and lime wedge to serve.

	CALORIES	SUGARS	FAT	SATURATED FAT	SALT
PER SERVING	1 cal (kcal)	0 g	0 g	0 g	0.01 g
GDA	0%	0%	0%	0%	0%

Apple Warmer

SERVES 4

3¾ cups (900 ml/30 fl oz) Coca-Cola*
3¾ cups (900 ml/30 fl oz) apple juice
4 tablespoons soft brown sugar
2 tablespoons whole cloves
1 teaspoon ground nutmeg
4 cinnamon sticks, to decorate

This lightly spiced punch is great for all ages and only takes a few minutes to prepare.

Combine all ingredients in a saucepan and bring slowly to a boil. Simmer gently for 30 seconds, then strain into a pitcher or jug. Use a ladle to pour into cups, mugs, or heatproof glasses and decorate each with a cinnamon stick.

	CALORIES	SUGARS	FAT	SATURATED FAT	SALT
PER SERVING	252 cal (kcal)	63.2 g	0.5 g	0.2 g	0 g
GDA	13%	70%	1%	1%	0%

Alcohol-free Eggnog

SERVES 1

½ cup (125 ml/4 fl oz) Coca-Cola®
½ cup (125 ml/4 fl oz) milk
1 teaspoon vanilla extract
2 eggs
3 tablespoons granulated sugar
¼ teaspoon ground cinnamon
¼ teaspoon ground nutmeg, plus extra
    for dusting
ice cubes

This alcohol-free version of the deliciously creamy classic Christmas tipple uses Coke® for a tasty twist.

Place all ingredients except the ice cubes in a blender and process until smooth. Fill an old-fashioned glass halfway with ice and pour the eggnog mixture over the ice. Dust the top with extra nutmeg and serve.

	CALORIES	SUGARS	FAT	SATURATED FAT	SALT
PER SERVING	522 cal (kcal)	78 g	16.4 g	6.5 g	0.5 g
GDA	26%	87%	23%	32%	8%

Index

Picture Credits

All images courtesy of The Coca-Cola Company with exception of the following:

Advertising Archives 32, 41 above, 58 right, 68 left, 41 centre, 42 above, 43, 48 right, 56 right, 58 left, 59 left, 60, 62 right, 63 left, 64 left & right, 65 above left & right, 68 right, 69 left & right.

Alamy Interfoto 21 below; Buddy Mays 26 above; Jeff Morgan13 17 below; Stream Images 22.

Corbis 8 above left, 11; Bettmann 14 above; CinemaPhoto 24 centre; Sygma 10 above; John Van Hasselt/Sygma 8 below right.

Getty Images Apic 17 above; Steve Granitz/ WireImage 42 below; Chris Graythen 23; Transcendental Graphics 39 left.

Octopus Publishing Group Lis Parsons 73–123.

The Kobal Collection Dreamworks Pictures 25 right; MGM 24 left; Warner Bros 25 centre.

TopFoto Topham Picturepoint 24.